W9-ABX-448

This Book is Presented To

_____

By

_____

Date

_____

Home Style Flavor

With

Flair!

By Alison DuBois Scutte

Dedications

I would like to dedicate this book to:

My Mother, Elizabeth DuBois, for teaching me how to cook and for instilling in me the love and the art of food and the confidence to pursue it.

Al Scutte III, for encouraging me to keep with it, helping me with the publishing, marketing and sales and for being the best husband in the world!

Our children, Merritt, Maxwell, Josie and Ryann for always eating what I cook and for being gentle critics when the meals were not book-worthy!

HSN, for allowing me to practice my craft and giving me the opportunity to write this book.

The Rosensweigs' for trusting in me and having the faith to place the Bravetti line of products in my hands!

Al and Carol Scutte for being the best in-laws I could hope for and for backing my book!

Home Style Flavor with Flair!

Published by

TV Demo's Inc.
10 Foxfire Lane
Oldsmar, FL 34677
Copy Right © 2002

ISBN 0-9727252-0-2

All rights reserved. No part of this book may be reproduced or transmitted in any form or by any means, electronic or mechanical, including photography and recording, or by any information retrieval system, without written permission from the publisher.

Printed by
Rose Printing Company, Inc.
Tallahassee, Florida

Photography & Food Styling by
Elizabeth M. DuBois
Alfred Scutte III
Alison D. Scutte

Manufactured in the United States of America
First Printing: 2003   10,000 copies

Table of Contents

Introduction

Hi! I hope you will enjoy your new cookbook!

Cooking for television is very different than cooking at home. Food for camera is usually all about looks...not taste! However, on HSN, the taste also matters because the show hosts, producers and crew like to eat and I can't stand to disappoint them with bland, plastic-tasting foods. So, my on-air recipes have melded into my home-cooked recipes and that union resulted into this book! It is a collection of my favorite recipes that I cook for my family and friends at home, as well as on the Home Shopping Network!

This book has a wide variety of recipes because I have a wide range of moods! You will find fun foods, fancy foods, light meals and family feasts. There are also many cultural variances in the mix; Asian, Italian, Cuban, Spanish and All-American dishes are included! My hope is that no matter your mood, something in this book will appeal to your palette.

People often ask me how I became a culinary product demonstrator on HSN. I began my career, not on camera, but as a Food Stylist behind the scenes. When I was in my teens, I had the opportunity to apprentice with a very talented, and sought-after, Food Stylist...my Mother! I assisted her on shoots for television commercials, magazines and grocery stores flyers and learned some tricks of the trade like how to use paint and blow torches to make a frozen turkey look cooked and delicious, how to mix colors and textures on the plate for appeal, how to pick the perfect tomato or shrimp for camera and how to be very meticulous! I once had to use tweezers and glue to put all the sesame seeds on a hamburger bun so that it looked perfect for a photograph!

Eventually, I became a Food Stylist on my own rights and from there, moved into on-air demonstration and I love it! I have demonstrated products and/or Food Styled on television in the US, Canada, London and Germany, but my favorite place is HSN!

The people are happy and fun to work with and they have become my second family. That is why, when I make up my demonstrations and prepare the foods, I want to make sure they taste good! I want Chris, Shannon, Lynn, Callie and the other hosts, to look forward to biting into the foods I am making with my products!

Although the foods I show on-air are not fake or painted, I do employ some Food Styling techniques to make them as appealing as possible. I have included many of these tips throughout the book so that you will not only be able to make delicious tasting meals, but also make them as attractive as possible!

However, when you make things at home, you can go a little slower and don't have to worry that a camera will pick up all of your mistakes! Mistakes do happen, especially on live TV!

Once, while in Canada demonstrating an Immersion Blender, I draped a tablecloth across a flat cook top to use under my product display. While I was making mayonnaise with my immersion blender, the host leaned onto the cloth, turned on the cook top and the whole set caught fire! They cut the cameras off the fire but left on my audio. I had to continue talking to the viewers while making my mayonnaise until they could put out the fire, remove the burned cloth and come back to us. My mayonnaise was so thick by then you could have used it as wallpaper paste!

Another time I was in Germany cooking turkey for my friend Denis Spanek who was on-air presenting his turkey roaster. The legs of the turkeys in Germany are extraordinarily long and thus hung over the edge of the pan. Grease from the legs dripped down into the oven, started a fire and the German Fire Brigade was called! As Denis was on-air, the firemen, complete with hats and picks, came running through to put out the fire! The station was fined and I was forever known as the "American Fire Devil"!

All in all, cooking on live TV is fun, but not without it's uncertainties! However, I would not trade it for the world!

Enjoy Your Book and Happy Cooking!

Breakfast & Brunch

To begin your day
Nutritionally right,
Treat yourself
To a breakfast delight!

Homemade Doughnuts

You know the doughnuts that are light and fluffy with a glaze all over them; the kind that people line up for at the doughnut shops? You can make them yourself at home!

2 cups lukewarm milk
2 packages yeast
½ cup sugar
1 teaspoon salt
½ cup shortening (Crisco)
2 eggs beaten
7 cups flour

Heat the milk in a 4-cup measuring cup, in the microwave, until just warm; add yeast and let dissolve. Add the sugar and salt to the yeast and stir.

In a large mixing bowl, cream the shortening with the eggs using your hand mixer. Pour in the liquid mixture, scraping all the sugar from the bottom of the cup, and mix well on the lowest speed. Using your dough hooks, slowly add the flour to the mixing bowl and mix until a soft dough-ball is formed. Cover with a clean towel and let rise until double in size.

Place dough on a very lightly floured surface and roll to ½-inch thick. Cut into rounds using a doughnut cutter. Remove unused dough from around the rings and let rings rise for 30 minutes. Fry in 1-inch hot oil or in your deep fryer, turning once, until golden brown. Drain and glaze!

Doughnut Glaze

2 cups sugar
½ cup butter
¾ cup milk
1 teaspoon vanilla

Cook the ingredients together over medium heat. When you can drop a little of the mixture into cold water and it forms a soft ball, the glaze is ready. Dip the drained dough nuts into glaze and let dry on a wire rack.

Easy Doughnut Glaze

2 cups powdered sugar
½ cup evaporated milk
water

Mix the sugar and milk together. Add water, drop by drop, until you get the desired consistency.

Cinnamon French Toast

French Toast doesn't have to be boring! Try this recipe using a good white bread from the bakery section of your favorite grocery sliced 1" thick; you'll think you are eating breakfast out!

8 slices of 1" thick white bread; or see variations below
4 eggs
¼ cup milk
½ teaspoon cinnamon
pinch nutmeg
butter flavored non-stick cooking spray
confectioners sugar

Place the eggs, milk, cinnamon and nutmeg into a bowl large enough to dip the bread slices in. Whisk together very well.

Preheat large non-stick skillet over medium heat. Spray lightly with a butter-flavored non-stick spray.

Start by dipping 4 slices of bread, one at a time, into the whipped egg mixture coating well; re-whisk after every other slice. Place into preheated pan. Cook until golden brown on the bottom, about 1 ½ - 2 minutes, and then turn. When both sides are golden, transfer to a serving platter. Sprinkle lightly with confectioner sugar. Repeat with remaining slices of bread.

Serve with butter and a good maple syrup.

Hint: If you must use a stainless steel pan, preheat the pan with a thin layer of vegetable oil and omit the cooking spray.

Variation: Use Cinnamon-Raisin, Whole Wheat or French bread instead of white!

Breakfast Sausage Patties

Try this delicious, lower-fat version of traditional store-bought breakfast sausage! Try serving them sandwiched between Southern-Style Biscuits with the cheese option; heavenly!

1 lb. Boneless Country Style Ribs
¼ tsp. rubbed sage
¼ tsp. marjoram
¼ tsp. coriander
1 tsp. salt
½ tsp. ground black pepper

Install the chopping blade inside your Bravetti 800 Watt Platinum Pro Food Processor; attach lid. Turn the processor on and set to speed 9. Drop the ribs, on at a time, through the feed shoot and process until smooth. Add the seasonings and continue processing on a medium speed until well blended.

Form into patties and fry in pan over medium heat.

Makes 1 lb.; about 7 patties.

Variation: increase the coriander to ½ teaspoon for a hotter version!

Southern-Style Biscuits

Traditional biscuits of the South use Buttermilk to make them light and fluffy. If you do not have buttermilk, use the variation recipe at the bottom of the page.

2 cups all-purpose flour
¾ tsp salt
3 teaspoons baking powder
1 teaspoon baking soda
4 tablespoons shortening
1 cup buttermilk (if not using, follow variation recipe below)
6 oz. sharp cheddar cheese (optional)

Cheese Option: using the thin shredding blade attached to your Food Processor, shred the cheese, then remove the shredding blade and insert the dough blade and proceed as directed below.

Using the dough blade attachment in your food processor, add all ingredients, except the buttermilk, and process lightly using your pulse button. When ingredients are mixed well, turn processor onto lowest speed and pour buttermilk slowly into the food shoot, adjusting the speed faster as needed.

Remove dough and place onto a lightly floured board. Roll it out to about a ½ inch thickness. Cut the dough with a biscuit, or round cookie, cutter and place onto a well-greased pan.

Bake for 15 minutes in a 425° pre-heated oven.

Variation Recipe: If you do not have buttermilk, use the following ingredients instead and follow the directions above!

2 cups all-purpose flour
½ teaspoon salt
2 teaspoons sugar
4 teaspoons baking powder
½ teaspoon cream of tartar
½ cup shortening
2/3 cup milk

Sausage Gravy Over Biscuits

You may use your Homemade or Store Bought sausage or simply buy the brown and serve patties to make this hearty breakfast treat!

1 lb. bulk breakfast sausage (store-bought or homemade)
3 tablespoons butter
2 ½ - 3 tablespoons flour
1 ½ cups milk, milk and cream, or half 'n half
¼ teaspoon salt
½ teaspoon coarse-ground black pepper
¼ teaspoon ground sage

Place the sausage in a large skillet over medium heat and cook until sausage is done and well browned; use your spatula to "chop" the sausage into bite size bits while cooking. Drain thoroughly on paper towels.

Gravy: Melt the butter, in a medium saucepan, over low heat. Add the flour and stir constantly for 3 to 4 minutes or until well blended and the taste of raw flour has vanished.

Slowly stir in the milk and seasonings. Simmer and stir the sauce with a wire whisk until it has thickened and is smooth and hot. Add the sausage crumbles and cook, stirring frequently, until the mixture just begins to boil. Remove from heat and ladle over hot, halved biscuits.

Hint: Serve with the Southern-Style Biscuits, see recipe index, but omit the cheese!

Food Styling Tip

To make this dish more attractive, save out some of the larger sausage crumbles to sprinkle onto of the individual plates of Sausage Gravy on Biscuits and then sprinkle a little Paprika on top!

Bacon, Mushroom, Spinach & Swiss Quiche

Quiches are delicious, great for any meal and surprisingly easy! Try this recipe, or the variations below, to impress guests and family!

¼ lb. sliced bacon
1 Tbsp. butter
½ cup sliced mushrooms
¼ cup chopped frozen spinach, thawed and patted dry
2 cups half 'n half
3 eggs
¼ tsp. salt
dash white pepper
½ cup diced or shredded Swiss cheese
1 9" ready to bake piecrust

Let the piecrust sit out of the refrigerator for 15 minutes to soften. Unfold and press into a 9" deep pie tin.

Fry the bacon in a skillet until it is almost done, drain on paper towel, chop and set aside. Add butter and mushrooms to the skillet with the bacon drippings and cook gently about 3 minutes. Add spinach and the chopped bacon and cook just until heated; remove from heat.

Pour half 'n half into a 4-6 cup glass measuring cup or bowl; microwave for 1 ½ minutes. Remove from microwave and blend in the eggs, salt and pepper; use the balloon whisk attachment of your Bravetti 300-Watt hand mixer and whisk until eggs are completely incorporated into the half 'n half.

Sprinkle the bacon/mushroom/spinach mixture and the cheese evenly onto the bottom of the piecrust. Pour egg mixture over it.

Bake at 375° for 35 to 40 minutes or until the top is golden brown. Slice and serve.

Variations: You can use 1 cup of any combination of meats and veggies and ½ cup of cheeses you like! Try using sausage and onion with cheddar cheese, or ham and blanched asparagus with Swiss; use your imagination, it's fun!

● ●

Breakfast Burritos

I love to make this because it is easy, delicious and can use virtually any leftovers and veggies I have in the fridge! Customize the filling to your likings!

2 tablespoons butter
2 tablespoons vegetable oil
½ cup sliced mushrooms
¼ cup finely chopped onion
1 can whole peeled potatoes; diced
½ cup ham, bacon or sausage; pre-cooked, drained and diced
½ cup tomatoes; seeded and chopped fine
6 eggs; well beaten with 2 tablespoons water
1 cup shredded cheddar cheese
4 large tortillas
salsa
sour cream

Melt the butter and the vegetable oil together over medium-low heat in a large skillet. Add the onions and mushrooms and sauté for about 3 minutes. Add the potatoes and continue cooking for another few minutes. Stir in the meat until heated throughout.

Pour the whipped eggs into the meat and veggie skillet and add the cheese. Cook, stirring frequently until the eggs start to set; add tomatoes. Continue cooking until the eggs are cooked and the cheese is melted and incorporated into the egg mixture. Remove from heat.

Place the tortillas on top of a damp paper towel, cover with another. Place into microwave and cook for 40 seconds. Remove hot tortillas; fill and roll with the egg mixture.

Place filled tortillas, seam side down, on plates and top with salsa and sour cream, if desired.

Eggs Benedict

This stunning dish is always delicious and can be made at home quite easily, especially if you have an egg poacher!

8 eggs
butter
½ tsp. salt
¼ tsp. white pepper
4 English Muffins
8 Slices Canadian Bacon
1 Cup Hollandaise Sauce

Split, toast and butter the English Muffins. Put onto platter or individual plates.

Lightly fry the Canadian bacon in a medium skillet over medium-high heat and place one slice onto each of the buttered muffin halves.

Poach the eggs in buttered poaching cups for about 4 minutes, or until whites have solidified and yolks are runny-firm.

Place the poached eggs atop the Canadian bacon on the muffins, sprinkle with salt and pepper. Cover with Hollandaise Sauce; see index for the recipe. Serve and enjoy!

To Poach an Egg without an Egg-Poacher:

Put 2 inches if water into a large skillet. You may want to add a little vinegar (1 tablespoon vinegar to 1 quart water) to keep the egg whites together; but just a bit as more vinegar will spoil the taste!

Bring the water to a full boil. Break each egg into a cup. Holding the rim just below the water's surface, slide the egg into the bubbling area so the bubbles spin the egg and sets the white around the yolk. Add up to 6 eggs to the pan. Immediately lower the heat so the water barely shivers. Cook the eggs, uncovered, for about 4 minutes or until whites have solidified and yolks are runny-firm. Remove eggs with slotted spoon and trim their edges with scissors. Drain for an instant on a folded paper towel. Season and serve.

Home Fried Potatoes

I boil my potatoes first to jump start the cooking process. That way, when they are fried, they will be cooked tender inside without getting overdone on the outside.

4 large red potatoes; diced into 1-inch cubes
¼ cup green onion; chopped (optional)
¼ cup green or red peppers; chopped (optional)
1 teaspoon salt
¼ teaspoon black pepper
2 tablespoons oil
1 tablespoon butter
¼ teaspoon paprika

Scrub and chop the potatoes and place them in a pot of rapidly boiling water. Boil for 5-6 minutes or until they are almost fork tender; drain.

Heat the oil in a large skillet over medium heat. When the oil is hot add the potatoes and spread in a layer in the pan. Cook 3-4 minutes or until they begin the brown. Add the salt, pepper, onion and peppers and stir well. Continue cooking until the potatoes are brown and the onion and peppers are tender. Sprinkle paprika over all and toss well.

Serve hot!

Food Styling Tip

To make these potatoes look nice...handle them gently! While frying, turn them gently so as not to tear the skins off or mash the potatoes. Also, use both red and green peppers and chop them coarsely so the colors will show up nicely. On-air, I actually cook the peppers separately from the potatoes and then just stir them together at the last minute!

Apple Pancakes

A delicious change from the ordinary!

1 cup flour
4 tablespoons sugar
2 teaspoons baking powder
½ teaspoon salt
¼ teaspoon cinnamon
¾ cup milk
2 tablespoons vegetable oil
1 egg
2-3 medium tart apples
½ tablespoon lemon juice
Non-stick cooking spray

Using a hand grater, grate the apples on the larger grate/shred side, until you have 1 cup. Squeeze ½ tablespoon lemon juice over the apples. Toss and set aside.

In a mixing bowl, mix together the dry ingredients. Add the oil, milk and egg and blend together using the lowest speed of your Bravetti hand mixer. When all of the large lumps are gone, use a wooden spoon and fold in the apples.

Heat griddle or non-stick skillet, over medium heat, until a drop of water will bounce and sputter. Spray pan with non-stick cooking spray. Spoon the batter onto the pan, spreading cakes to get the size you want; don't overcrowd. When the entire cake is bubbly and the bubbles on the edge begin to break open (about 2 to 3 minutes), turn the cakes. Turn only once! The second side won't take as long so watch for it to be golden brown.

Serve with powdered sugar or syrup.

Hint: This recipe makes about 12 small pancakes so double it if you have a hungry crowd!

Monte Cristo Sandwiches

These are fantastic, especially when you can't decide if you want breakfast or lunch!

8 slices white bread
8 slices baked ham; medium-thin
8 slices Swiss cheese; thin
Butter to spread
4 eggs
2 tablespoon water
Non-stick cooking spray
Confectioners sugar
Maple syrup

Make sandwiches by putting two slices ham between two slices Swiss cheese and two buttered slices white bread. Use your hand to mash the sandwich until the bread is about as half as thick as it was.

In a mixing bowl large enough to dip the sandwiches, beat egg and water with the whisk attachment of your Bravetti hand mixer until frothy.

Heat large skillet over medium heat. Spray with cooking spray. Dip sandwiches, one at a time, into the frothy egg until completely covered. Place into heated skillet and cook for 2-3 minutes on each side or until golden brown and cheese has melted.

Place on individual plates and cut into 4 triangle pieces. Sprinkle with confectioners sugar and serve with individual small bowls of syrup for dipping.

Fresh Fruit Smoothie

A refreshing treat for breakfast, brunch or anytime!

1 cup vanilla flavored yogurt
½ cup cubed honeydew
½ cup cubed cantaloupe
½ cup cubed watermelon
1 cup vanilla flavored yogurt
½ cup milk
½ cup ice
2 teaspoons of sugar or honey; or 1packet sugar substitute

Place all ingredients, in order given, into your Bravetti Blender or the blender attachment on your Bravetti Platinum-Pro Food Processor. Blend until smooth; enjoy!

Variation: Try using different flavors of yogurt, adding wheat germ or trying strawberries, blueberries, raspberries or any of your favorite fruits to make this your own signature smoothie!

Food Styling Tip

I always make sure that one of the fruits has a vibrant color; strawberry, raspberry or blueberry work nice. That way the drink looks as good as it tastes! Plus I save a few berries to place on top of the drink and I add a straw!

Blueberry Muffins

The smell of these alone is worth the little bit of effort it takes to make these summer-time treats! Of course you can always use frozen to make your summer year-round!

2 cups flour
3 tablespoons sugar
1 tablespoon baking powder
¼ teaspoon salt
1 cup milk
1 egg
3 tablespoons melted butter or margarine
1 cup fresh blueberries; washed and dried

In a medium mixing bowl, mix together the dry ingredients. In a smaller bowl, mix together the milk, egg and butter using a wire whisk. Pour the wet ingredients into the dry and mix together with a wooden spoon just enough to moisten the batter; it should remain lumpy. Fold in the blueberries being careful not to break them.

Fill greased muffin cups 2/3 full and bake at 400° for about 20 minutes.

Makes 12 medium or 24 small muffins.

<u>Food Styling Tip</u>

Don't mix all of the blueberries into the batter! Save some to sprinkle onto of the batter after you have poured it into the muffin tin, them gently press them lightly into the batter so that they will remain visible once baked!

Zucchini Nut Bread

If you have trouble getting your kids to eat their veggies...try
spreading butter on a hot slice of this bread and watch them smile!

3 eggs
1 cup oil
2 cups sugar
2 cups finely shredded raw zucchini
2 teaspoons vanilla
3 cups flour
1 teaspoon salt
1 teaspoon baking powder
1 teaspoon baking soda
1 teaspoon cinnamon
¼ teaspoon nutmeg
1 ½ cup chopped nuts

In a large mixing bowl, beat the eggs. Add the oil, sugar, zucchini
and vanilla and mix well. Combine the dry ingredients and mix
them into the egg mixture until well blended.
Stir in nuts.

Pour into 2 greased loaf pans and bake at 325° for 1 hour.

Sour Cream Banana Nut Bread

This is the best banana nut bread I've ever had! It makes two loaves for good reason...you just can't stop eating it! Of course you can always give one loaf away to save your waistline and make a life-long friend at the same time!

½ cup butter or margarine; softened
2 cups sugar
4 eggs
2 teaspoons vanilla
3 cups flour
2 teaspoons baking soda
¼ teaspoon salt
3 cups mashed ripe bananas
1 cup sour cream
1 cup chopped walnuts

Lightly grease and flour 2 loaf pans.

Use your Bravetti hand mixer and cream butter and sugar together in a medium mixing bowl. Add eggs and vanilla and beat for one full minute.

Add the dry ingredients and continue mixing, on lowest speed, until well blended.

Add bananas, sour cream and nuts and continue mixing, on medium, until smooth.

Pour into prepared loaf pans and bake at 350° for 1 hour or until done. The sour cream makes this bread so moist that the toothpick will not come out entirely clean!

Cinnamon Rolls

I can't think of anything better than warm chewy, gooey, homemade cinnamon rolls! They take a little work but they are worth it!

2 ¼ oz. packets dry yeast	5 cups flour
1 teaspoon salt	½ cup butter, softened
½ cup sugar	½ cup sugar
1 egg	1 tablespoon cinnamon
1/3 cup cooking oil	
2 cups warm water	

Vanilla Glaze

2 ½ tablespoons half & half, cream or milk
¼ teaspoon vanilla
1 tablespoon butter, softened
1 ½ to 2 cups powdered sugar
pinch of salt

In your Bravetti Blender, put yeast, salt, sugar, egg, oil and warm water and blend well. Place flour into a large mixing bowl, pour in yeast mixture and mix well. Cover and let rise to double; about 1 hour. Punch down.

Mix together the butter, sugar and cinnamon; set aside.

Working with half the dough at a time, place dough onto lightly floured board and roll to ½ inch thickness. Spread half of the cinnamon mixture evenly on the dough. Roll the dough and slice into 1 ½ inch pieces. Place onto a well-greased round 9 inch cake pan.

Repeat with the other half of the dough. Allow both pans to rise to double again; about 30 minutes.

Bake in a pre-heated 350° oven for 18-20 minutes. Remove from oven and immediately take rolls out of pans to cool.

Put the glaze ingredients into your blender and blend until smooth; add a little more powdered sugar for a thicker glaze. Spread onto the almost-cooled cinnamon rolls.

• •

Peppers and Eggs Sandwiches

This recipe came to me from my sister-in-law, Alecia. She learned how to make this delicious dish from an older Italian man she used to work with, Nick DePalma. She says he reminded her of Santa Claus! My thanks to Santa, and Alecia, because my husband absolutely loves this dish for lunch...and he usually does not like peppers!

1 dozen eggs
1 small yellow onion; finely chopped
1/2 cup grated Parmesan cheese
6 large green peppers; diced into small squares
salt
pepper
olive oil
4-6 Round or long rolls

In large frying pan, cover bottom of pan with olive oil and heat over medium. When oil is hot, add the peppers and cook, covered, until tender but not mushy.

Beat eggs in a medium mixing bowl, with a fork, until well blended. Add the cheese and sprinkle with salt and pepper.

Right before peppers are done add onion to the pan and cook, with the peppers, until tender; just one or two minutes as onions don't take long to get tender. Drain excess olive oil from pan and return to stove. Add eggs and cook until firm; stirring occasionally. Taste, and add more salt and pepper as desired.

Put peppers and eggs on rolls and serve hot.

Alecia's Note: If people have problems eating peppers because they repeat on them, make sure the peppers are well done and they won't you repeat on you.

Al's Apple Cake

This recipe comes from my husband Al's family, but it is so delicious and beautiful that it has become one of my family's absolute favorite cakes for morning, noon and night! After it is a day old, we warm it slightly and spread it with butter for a wonderful treat. Al did not want to part with the recipe, but I finally convinced him to share it! Thank you, Sweetheart!

3 cups flour
2 cups sugar
3 teaspoons baking powder
4 large eggs
1 cup oil
1 teaspoon vanilla
½ cup orange juice

3 large, or 5-6 small, red apples (we use Gala or Golden Delicious)
3 tablespoons cinnamon
4 tablespoons sugar
1 teaspoon nutmeg

In a large mixing bowl, combine the flour, 2 cups of sugar and baking powder. Add in the eggs, oil, vanilla and orange juice and mix with a hand mixer until smooth. Set aside.

Peel, core and thinly slice the apples; place into a plastic zip-close bag. In a small bowl, combine the cinnamon, sugar and nutmeg. Sprinkle the spice mixture over the apples and toss in the bag until all the apples are well coated.

Prepare the inside of the Bundt pan by lightly greasing the entire surface, making sure you get into all the grooves, and flouring it. Shake off all excess flour.

Pour half of the batter into the pan. Place half of the apples in a layer over the batter. Pour over the remaining batter and top with the remaining apples.

Bake at 350° for 75 minutes. Or...*Variation:* Use two 1 ½ - pound loaf pans instead of the bundt pan and bake for 60 minutes.

● ●

Appetizers, Dips & Finger Foods

Before you serve the promised meal,
A savory snack has great appeal!

Hummus

I never really liked Hummus until, at Darlene Cahill's suggestion, I made up this recipe to demonstrate my Bravetti Do-It-All on HSN. Now, I love Hummus! I must not be alone because everyone gobbles this up after the show! Maybe it'll change your mind too!

1 can chickpeas; drained
1 1 ½ oz. jar chopped pimentos
10 jumbo pitted black olives
3 large cloves garlic
3 large basil leaves
¼ cup extra virgin olive oil
½ tsp. salt
1 tablespoon lemon juice

Place all ingredients in your Bravetti Platinum-Pro Food Processor or Do-It-All. Process on the highest speed until well blended and creamy. Serve with whole-wheat pita wedges, flat bread cut into wedges or melba toast.

Spicy Black Bean Dip

This is a great tasting dip for any get together! Plus, it's always nice to offer a vegetarian alternative at parties.

1 14 oz. can black beans; drained
½ cup sour cream
2 cloves garlic
½ tsp. cumin
½ tsp. salt
3 green onions, whites and 1" greens
1 teaspoon lemon juice
1 small can chopped green chilies
2 green onions, whites and 2" greens thinly sliced

Place all ingredients, except final 2 green onions, in the large chopper bowl of your Bravetti Do-It-All II or your Bravetti 600 Watt Food Processor. Process until smooth. Spoon into bowl and sprinkle remaining green onions on top. Serve with tortilla chips and guacamole, if desired.

Guacamole

There are many versions to this traditional Mexican topping. Some restaurants make the recipe go further by adding sour cream, cream cheese or mayo. I prefer it straight, but if the avocados are expensive in your area and you have to serve a crowd, go ahead and add one of the above-mentioned expanders!

2 large ripe avocados; peeled and seed removed
½ lemon
½ teaspoon cayenne pepper
½ teaspoon Worcestershire sauce
¼ teaspoon salt, or more to taste
1 tablespoon grated onion (optional)
2 tablespoons tomato, seeded and finely chopped (optional)

Peel, remove seed and slice or cube avocado; put into a small mixing bowl. Add spices and squeeze lemon over all being mindful of the lemon's seeds. Mix all ingredients, except tomato, together until creamy using the traditional beaters of your Bravetti 300 Watt Hand Mixer or mash with a fork. Fold in the tomatoes.

Serve alone with tortilla chips or along with salsa and/or spicy black bean dip.

Hint: Try making the tortilla chips yourself using your Bravetti Flash Fryer!

Food Styling Tip

When making guacamole, you must handle it extremely gently or it will bruise. Choose an avocado that is soft to the touch, but not too mushy. Use plenty of lemon after every cut and make it just before serving for best results! If you must store it for more than an hour, place plastic wrap directly on the dip to keep out as much air as possible! To serve, place the dip in a bright colored bowl and top with a wedge of lemon and some finely chopped tomato.

Spicy Fresh Salsa

Polls have shown that Salsa is America's favorite condiment...it even beats out ketchup in popularity! Here is the recipe I use on HSN while demonstrating choppers and food processors. Everyone must love it because even during 5 am shows, the show host, producer and crew eat it up! I just have to make sure the chips are fresh!

6 medium plum tomatoes (ends trimmed; halved)
½ medium-large white onion (halved)
1 medium jalapeno; stem and seeds removed
½ bunch cilantro; large stems removed
½ tsp. Salt
½ tsp. cumin
5½ oz. can spicy V-8 juice

Place all ingredients into food processor with chopping blade. Use the pulse button intermittently to chop mixture to desired consistently.

Serve with tortilla chips.

Hint: Try making the tortilla chips yourself using your Bravetti Flash Fryer!

Mexican 9 Layer Dip

This is definitely a party favorite. I like to take it to get-togethers because no one else ever brings it but there are always chips!

1 ½ lbs. ground meat
1 teaspoon salt
1 ½ tablespoons flour
1 ½ tablespoons chili powder

1 ½ cups water
½ teaspoon cumin
½ teaspoon garlic powder

In skillet, sauté meat until brown and crumbly; drain and return meat to skillet. Sprinkle the salt, flour and chili powder evenly over meat. Add water, cumin and garlic powder. Cook over medium until thickened. Set aside to use as the meat layer during assembly.

2 16-ounce cans refried beans
3 large avocados
¼ teaspoon pepper
2 tablespoons lemon juice
½ teaspoon salt
1 ½ cups sour cream
2 tablespoons chili powder; or more to taste
1 cup chopped green onions with tops
1 ½ cups thinly shredded iceberg lettuce
2 large tomatoes, seeded and chopped
2 41/4-ounce cans sliced black olives
2 cups thinly shredded sharp cheddar or Mexican Blend cheese
1 small jar pickled jalapeno slices, if desired

Heat refried beans until hot and spread evenly in a greased 9x13-inch serving dish.

In a small bowl, mash the avocado with the pepper and lemon juice until smooth. Spread evenly over warm beans. Sprinkle taco meat evenly over the avocado layer. Next, mix together the sour cream, chili powder and green onions; spread over the taco meat. Then add the shredded lettuce followed by the chopped tomatoes, the black olives and then finally the cheese. Top with pickled jalapeno slices for an extra kick!

Serve while the beans and meat are still warm, or refrigerate until ready. Serve with sturdy tortilla chips.

● ●

Curry Dip for Veggies

This is a nice change from Ranch Salad Dressing! It is amazing what a little curry will do for mayonnaise!

1 cup mayonnaise (store bought or home made)
½ cup sour cream
¼ teaspoon ground ginger
1 clove garlic; minced
½ teaspoon salt
2 tablespoons green onion; chopped
1 ½ teaspoon curry powder; more to taste
lemon juice to taste

Place all ingredients into blender, except lemon juice. After all ingredients are thoroughly mixed, add lemon juice to taste. Serve with fresh vegetable sticks and pieces.

Hint: If you are making home made mayo using your Bravetti Immersion Blender, simply add the remaining ingredients, after the mayonnaise has thickened, and continue blending until smooth!

Food Styling Tip

When making any vegetable tray, arrange the vegetables by alternating colors! Don't place all of the green vegetables together, separate them with the carrots, broccoli, yellow pepper strips, etc. Make sure you line the tray with dark lettuce leaves or shredded iceberg and leave room for a colorful dip bowl in the middle!

Party Cheese Dip

I made originally up this recipe to demonstrate the power of the Bravetti hand mixer on HSN. As it turns out, it tastes great and so many viewers have requested it, I wanted to include it in my book!

1 8oz. block cream cheese
1 8oz. block Velveeta cheese
½ cup Blue cheese crumbles
3 thinly sliced green onions with tops
1 small jar chopped pimento; drained
2 tsp. garlic salt
2 tsp. Worcestershire sauce

Use your Bravetti hand mixer with the traditional beaters to blend these ingredients into a smooth creamy dip. Serve with crackers and celery stalks.

Food Styling Tip

When making this dip, you walk a fine line from a Food Stylist's point of view! You want the onions to show, but don't want a bite of dip to be overwhelming for the eater!
I omit the white part of the onion and use just the green tops; from the lightest green to half way up the darkest leaves. I slice the onions on a slight angle and make them about 1/8-inch wide. I also save some of the greenest leaves and about ½ - teaspoon chopped pimento to sprinkle on top!

Pimento Cheese stuffed Celery Bites

My Grandmother always included this on our Thanksgiving table's relish tray, but they were often gone before dinner started! On HSN, Chris Scanlon is a big fan of this recipe! In fact, when I changed my Food Processor demonstration and omitted it, she seemed so disappointed that I put it back in!

1 bunch celery, washed and large end removed
1 lb. Block Sharp cheddar cheese
1/3 cup mayonnaise (homemade is best)
1 Tbsp. Vinegar
¼ tsp. Dry mustard
¼ tsp. Worcestershire
½ tsp. Salt
½ tsp. pepper
1 ½ oz. Jar chopped pimento; drained

Using the small shredding blade of your Bravetti Food Processor, shred cheese. Remove shredding blade; insert dough blade.

In a small bowl, mix together the mayonnaise, vinegar, dry mustard, Worcestershire, salt and pepper until well blended. Add the mayonnaise mixture along with the pimentos to the cheese inside the food processor bowl. Process on a medium speed for about 1 minute or until creamy.

Spread the cheese mixture into the celery ribs. Cut the stuffed ribs into 1 ½ - 2 inch pieces. Arrange on a platter and serve.

Food Styling Tip

Don't use the wide portion of the celery rib. Use only the uniformly wide part of the stalk. Stuff the entire stalk with the cheese and then cut it into 3 equal pieces.

Green Onion Roll-Ups

These are pretty on a tray and taste good too! Add them to your anti pasta tray!

3 bunches green onions, about 24 total
4-ounces spreadable cream cheese
1 tablespoon cracked black pepper
4-5 slices Deli thin-sliced pastrami
Bowl ice water

Wash and trim the roots from the green onions. Trim the tops leaving 3 inches of green. Using a sharp knife split each leaf in half length-wise. Place the onions into the bowl of ice water for about 10 minutes so that the leaves will curl.

Lay the pastrami out on a large cutting board. Spread the cream cheese thinly on the pastrami slices to completely cover; sprinkle with the black pepper.

Cut the pastrami into 1 ½-inch wide x 3-inch long strips; each slice of pastrami should yield 6 strips.

Remove the onions from the water and dry them. Lay the onions, one at a time, a top one end of a strip of the prepared pastrami. Roll the pastrami around the onion. Repeat until all onions are rolled.

Lay the onions on a small platter or stand on end with the curly leaves up to serve!

Food Styling Tip

To make this really pretty, trim the roots from the onions and all but 3-inches from the leaves. Use a sharp knife and split the leaves from the root out. Place them in a bowl of ice water for 10 minutes and they will curl. Pat them completely dry and then roll as directed above!

Mozzarella Stuffed Tomato Bites

These are a little time consuming to make but are an excellent addition to your party buffet as everyone seems to like them!

24 cherry tomatoes
½ lb. fresh mozzarella cheese
5-6 basil leaves; cut into thin strips
Balsamic vinegar
Good-quality extra-virgin olive oil
Italian seasoning

Using a sharp knife carefully slice off just the tops of the cherry tomatoes. Use the small end of a melon ball scoop to remove the insides of the tomatoes.

Cut the mozzarella cheese into cubes small enough to fit inside the tomatoes; set aside.

To assemble the tomatoes, start by spooning 1/8 teaspoon of balsamic vinegar inside the tomato and then set a cube of cheese inside. Drizzle very lightly with olive oil and then curl a strip of basil on top. Top with a sprinkling of Italian seasoning if desired.

Arrange the tomatoes on a small plate or serving platter.

These may be refrigerated for 2-3 hours before serving if covered tightly with plastic wrap.

Variation: to speed up making these use Roma tomatoes. Cut the tomatoes in half and use a melon baler to remove the seeds and meat then place cubes of mozzarella, basil leaves and balsamic vinegar as directed above.

Stuffed Black Olives

These taste like tacos without the shell! Kids love them as well as adults!

24 colossal black olives, pitted
8 ounces cream cheese
½ cup salsa; jar or fresh as hot as you like
1 cup thinly shredded iceberg lettuce

Using your hand mixer, combine the salsa and the cream cheese together until creamy.
Place into a clear sandwich bag and snip off one end to act as a pastry bag.

Pipe the mixture into the black olives.

Place the lettuce onto a small plate or serving platter and arrange the olives on top.

Variation: Instead of salsa, you may combine the cream cheese with any one or a combination of the following: chives, garlic salt, blue cheese crumbles, minced anchovies, tuna, diced picked jalapenos, smoked salmon or chopped almonds.

Spinach Dip in Pumpernickel

This dip is always well received at any party as well as on camera because it looks great! I also like it because I can make the dip a day or two ahead and assemble it just before the guests arrive.

1 10-ounce package frozen chopped spinach; thawed and drained
1 package Knorr's Swiss Vegetable Soup
1 cup mayonnaise
2 cups sour cream
1 8-ounce can water chestnuts; chopped
¼ cup green onions and tops; thinly sliced
1 round pumpernickel loaf (or sourdough); hollowed, reserving remaining bread for dipping
loaves of rye and pumpernickel for dipping cubes (see tip below)

In a medium glass bowl, mix all ingredients except bread. Cover bowl and chill for 6 hours, or up to 1 week. Spoon into hollowed pumpernickel round loaf. Cut remaining bread into squares and arrange around the spinach-filled bread for dipping.

Food Styling Tip

I always buy an extra loaf of pumpernickel and a loaf of rye bread to cut into cubes for the dipping. When I arrange the platter, I put the dip bowl on first and then place the bread cubes, alternating colors, around the bowl! I usually place a few cherry tomatoes around as well!

Antipasto Party Tray

You can't go wrong when you serve your guests a beautiful antipasti tray! This is practically a meal in itself!

Any good antipasti tray will offer a variety of meats, cheeses, vegetables and other tid bits. Depending on the size of your group, choose two or three meats and a couple of cheeses as the foundation of your tray.

Next choose a few vegetables. I usually pick 2 fresh, 2 marinated and 2 pickled. I usually buy my marinated vegetables and pickled selections in jars or from the deli section of my grocery, but you may marinade your own vegetables by covering them with Italian salad dressing and refrigerating them for 24 hours.

Finally complete your tray with a few select tidbits.

Suggested Meats and Cheeses:

Genoa Salami
Hard Salami
Pepperoni
Ham or Prosciutto
Roast Beef
Turkey Breast
Mozzarella
Provolone
Parmesan
Extra-Sharp Cheddar

Suggested Vegetables:

Fresh sliced tomatoes
Green onions
Radishes
Cucumber slices
Carrots
Roasted Red Peppers
Marinated Artichoke Hearts

● ●

Marinated Mushrooms
Marinated Garlic Olives
Peperoncini
Green Olives
Pickled beets

Tidbits:

Anchovies or Sardines
Tuna Salad
Smoked Salmon Slices
Crunchy Bread Sticks
Cheese Stuffed Celery
Melon wrapped with Prosciutto
Stuffed Black Olives
Mozzarella stuffed Cherry Tomatoes
Green Onion Roll-Ups

Assembling your tray:

Start by placing a bed of lettuce or spinach leaves on a large platter and then roll your deli-sliced meats and cube your cheeses into individual bite size pieces. Then arrange the slices and pieces attractively around the edge of a large platter. Finally arrange the vegetables and tidbits artfully in groups in the center of the platter.

For Serving/Assembling Ideas, see the photograph in the inserts.

Spicy Shrimp and Scallop Ceviche

This is kind-of-like a soup and kind-of-like a salad! Whatever it is, it's great!

1 lb. fresh shrimp; peeled, de-veined and chopped into small pieces
1 lb. fresh bay scallops
1 ¼ cup lime juice
½ cup finely chopped onion
1 cup chopped tomatoes
1 teaspoon chopped cilantro
¼ cup chopped green chilies
1 ½ cups V-8 juice
1 teaspoon Tabasco sauce
4 avocados; peeled, seeded and cut in half lengthwise
iceberg lettuce; shredded

In a glass bowl, marinade the shrimp and scallops in 1 cup of the lime juice for 2 hours in the refrigerator.

Drain the juice and add the onion, tomato, cilantro, chilies, V-8, remaining lime juice and Tabasco sauce. Chill for 2 hours.

Serve over avocado halves atop a bed of shredded lettuce or see tip below.

Food Styling Tip

*When serving this dish, I like to put it into martini or wide brim wine glasses!
I also save out 1 shrimp per serving to lay on the rim of the glass along with a thin wedge of lime. I place the glass on a saucer and garnish with spinach leaves or other lettuce and lay the spoon behind!*

Salmon Cheese Ball

I like to serve this because it's fancy enough to impress, but plain enough to taste great!

1 16-ounce can red salmon
1 teaspoon horseradish
4 teaspoons onion; finely chopped
1 teaspoon lemon juice
1 teaspoon Liquid Smoke
1 16-ounce block cream cheese; softened
½ cup fresh chopped parsley
1 cup sliced almonds or finely chopped pecans

Place salmon, horseradish, onion, lemon juice, Liquid Smoke and cream cheese into a medium mixing bowl. Use the traditional beaters of your Bravetti hand mixer and combine ingredients until smooth.

Roll the ingredients into a ball. Press the chopped parsley and nuts into the outside of the ball until completely covered.

Wrap tightly with clear wrap and store in the refrigerator for 1 hour or until ready to serve. Serve with crackers.

Food Styling Tip
To roll the mixture into a perfect sphere, I moisten my hands with water to keep it from sticking! I then spread the parsley and nuts on a sheet of clear plastic wrap and roll the ball around until it is covered. I use this same sheet to store the ball until I am ready to serve it.

Artichoke Spinach Dip

Variations of this dip are so popular that restaurants have even put it on their menus. However, it is very simple to make at home and serve anytime! I often make it when demonstrating the Bravetti Convection oven because it looks great and everyone loves to eat it after the show!

1 cup artichokes
1 10-ounce package frozen chopped spinach; thawed and drained
1 cup mayonnaise
1 8-ounce block cream cheese
1 cup grated Parmesan cheese
1 tablespoon lemon juice
½ teaspoon coarse ground black pepper
½ teaspoon paprika

Using your chopping blade of your food processor, process artichokes until well chopped. Remove the chopping blade and insert the dough blade. Add the spinach, mayonnaise, cream cheese, Parmesan cheese, lemon juice and black pepper. Process until smooth and well blended.

Spread mixture into a 9" square or 9"x11" baking dish. Sprinkle evenly with the paprika. Cook for 20 minutes at 350° or until hot and bubbly.

Serve hot with Melba toast or crackers.

Hint: For a large crowd, double the recipe and use your 3-quart slow cooker! Heat on high for 1 hour and then reduce heat to the keep warm setting; serve the dip directly from the slow cooker.

Sausage Balls

I always looked forward to family events because my Aunt Bonnie always made these! When I found out how easy they are, I started making them myself. You should give them a try and see if they become a favorite in your family.

1 ½ lb. roll Jimmy Dean® brand mild or medium sausage or use home made
1 cup Bisquick®
1 cup shredded cheddar cheese

Using the traditional beaters or the dough hooks of your Bravetti Hand Mixer, combine ingredients until completely mixed.

Roll into 1" balls and place on a jelly-roll pan.

Bake in a 375° oven for 15 minutes. Drain on paper towels and serve hot or at room temperature. Refrigerate leftovers.

Cheesy Rice Balls

My friend Julianne, who is a very talented food stylist and cake decorator for HSN, made these for me one time to use during a deep-fryer presentation. I thought they were so good, I decided to adopt her recipe and include it in my book. Try them for yourself and see how you like them!

4 ½ -ounces Minute Rice
3 tablespoons butter
3 tablespoons all-purpose flour
1 teaspoon salt
1/8 teaspoon ground white pepper
1/8 teaspoon cayenne
½ teaspoon dry mustard
1 cup milk
1 ½ cups finely grated sharp cheese
1 teaspoon Worcestershire
1 teaspoon grated onion
1 egg
2 cups dry breadcrumbs

Prepare rice according to directions. In a saucepan, melt the butter. Blend in flour, salt, pepper, cayenne and dry mustard. Gradually add milk, stirring constantly over low heat until mixture is very thick.

Add cheese, Worcestershire and onion; remove from heat and stir in rice. Chill mixture.

Roll into 1-inch balls. Dip each ball in slightly beaten egg and then roll in breadcrumbs.

Heat your Bravetti Flash Fryer to 375° and fry about 2 minutes or until golden brown. Drain on paper towels and serve warm.

Deviled Crab Croquettes

I first tasted deviled crabs at a little Cuban-style restaurant in Ybor City, FL. They closed up shop a couple of years ago and I was forced to learn to make my own! When I finally figured out how to make these delicious morsels, I wanted to share them with you!

3 tablespoons butter or margarine
3 tablespoons flour
1 cup milk
1 teaspoon salt
1/8 teaspoon pepper
¾ teaspoons dry mustard
¼ teaspoon Worcestershire
1/8 teaspoon Tabasco
1 tablespoon onion; finely grated
2 cups crabmeat
1 cup dry breadcrumbs
2 eggs; slightly beaten

Melt butter in a medium saucepan over low heat. Stir in flour to make a paste and then gradually add milk, stirring constantly until you have a thick cream sauce. Add all seasonings, onion and crab meat. Mix well and chill.

Make into balls; roll in bread crumbs, then beaten egg and then again in the bread crumbs. Fry at 375° in your Bravetti Flash Fryer, do not overcrowd, for about 2 minutes or until golden brown. Serve hot.

Hint: If you do not have a deep fryer, fry in a pan using very hot oil and turn often.

Spicy Buffalo-Style Chicken Wings

I can't believe there are so many restaurants dedicated to making these spicy munchies. They are very easy to make at home so...go for it! It's up to you if want to wear orange shorts and a tight T-shirt when you serve them!

1 ½ lb. Chicken Wings; separated, washed and patted dry

Breading:
1 cup flour
1 tsp. salt
1 tsp. Pepper
1 tsp. Paprika

Wing Sauce:
1 bottle Crystal brand cayenne pepper sauce
¼ Cup honey

Preheat your Bravetti Flash Fryer to 375°.

In small batches shake the wing segments with the flour, salt, pepper and paprika in a plastic bag or container until coated. Using metal tongs, gently drop wings into lowered basket of fryer; do not overcrowd. Fry, with lid on, for 8 minutes or until golden brown. Drain on paper towels and place in non-stick baking dish.

Heat wing sauce in small saucepan until warm. Pour desired amount of sauce over wings and bake in a 350° oven for 10-15 minutes.

Note: To prepare larger amounts, fry wings in 1 lb. increments, then place in 9 ½" x 11" pan. The wing sauce is enough to coat 3-4 lbs. Wings may be fried a day ahead, refrigerated, and then baked with the sauce for 25-30 minutes.

Green Olive Surprise

Your taste buds are in for a treat when you bite into these!

¼ cup soft butter
1 cup sharp cheddar cheese; grated
¼ teaspoon salt
¼ teaspoon paprika
¾ cup flour
3 dozen medium or large stuffed green olives

Use your hand mixer to cream the butter and cheese. Add the other ingredients, except olives, to form a dough. Chill dough for 15 minutes.

Using about 1 teaspoon dough for each olive, and form around olive; seal tightly. Bake at 400° for 12-15 minutes or until golden brown, or fry in your Bravetti Flash Fryer. Serve hot or cold.

Hawaiian Meatballs

Always a favorite! I often include these in my slow cooker presentations on HSN because they are so popular. I bet you'll like them too!

1 lb. lean ground beef
½ cup soft breadcrumbs moistened with milk
1 beaten egg
1 clove garlic; minced
½ teaspoon dry mustard
¼ teaspoon ginger
½ teaspoon salt
1 tablespoon soy sauce

Combine ingredients in a large mixing bowl. Form meat into 1-inch balls and sauté until brown in 2 tablespoons vegetable oil.

Pour over all: Sweet and Sour Sauce – Luau Style (see index for recipe).

Serve with white rice for dinner. Or for entertaining, place meatballs and sauce into a slow cooker on "keep warm" and have toothpicks ready!

Hint: If you do not have time to make the sauce from scratch, heat a bottled sauce together with 1 can drained pineapple tidbits and one chopped green pepper and pour over meatballs.

Oyster Stuffed Mushrooms

I always liked oyster stuffing, but not for the whole turkey! This makes a delicious pre-dinner snack for Thanksgiving and other holidays.

2 3 2/3-ounce cans smoked oysters; drained and chopped
2 lbs. fresh mushrooms; washed, stems removed and chopped
2 tablespoons butter; melted
4 tablespoons green onions; minced
1 cup sour cream
1 cup dry bread crumbs
3 tablespoons grated Parmesan cheese
a little milk to moisten stuffing

In a large mixing bowl, combine chopped mushroom stems, butter, onions, sour cream, bread crumbs, parmesan cheese and oysters. Add a little milk to moisten mixture if it appears dry.

Fill mushroom caps. Place caps into a 9"x13" baking dish. Bake at 375° for 15 to 20 minutes. Serve hot.

Variation: Substitute a 71/2-ounce can of white crabmeat for the oysters.

Shrimp Egg Rolls

Homemade egg rolls are easy to make and are a fun way to get the kids to help in the kitchen. You can make a whole batch, fry some to eat now and then freeze the rest for a later day.

2 cups salad shrimp, thawed and drained
1 cup celery, diced small or julienne
1 1/2 cups carrot, diced small or julienne
1/3 cup red pepper, minced fine
4 cups Chinese cabbage, shredded
2 tablespoons vegetable oil
4 tablespoons soy sauce, low sodium
1 teaspoon Chinese 5 spice
1/2 teaspoon salt
4 teaspoons potato starch
1/3 cup water
50 egg roll skins

In a large skillet, heat oil over medium heat. Add celery, carrots and red pepper. Sauté 1 minute. Add cabbage and 2 Tbs. soy sauce. Turning and stirring constantly, cook until cabbage is wilted; about 3 minutes. Mix in the 5 spice and cook another minute. Add the shrimp, remaining soy sauce and salt. Mix well and cook until shrimp are warmed; about 2 minutes.

In a small bowl, mix together the potato starch and water. Pour over the shrimp and veggies and mix well. Remove pan from heat and let stand 10 minutes.

Place a small amount of the shrimp/veggie mixture onto egg roll skin and wrap. See illustration for technique. Continue until all skins are used.

Note: Adjust the amount of mixture you use for each egg roll depending on the size and quantity you desire.

Preheat you Bravetti Flash Fryer to 430°. Fry the egg rolls in batches and drain on paper towels. Serve with sweet & sour dipping sauce.

Egg & Olive Finger Sandwiches

It's amazing what a little olive will do to your basic egg salad! When you serve this in small sandwiches with the crust cut off, they make beautiful sandwiches! Try alternating wheat and white bread for color.

3 hard boiled eggs
10 medium pimento-stuffed green olives
¼ tsp. dry mustard
¼ tsp. pepper
¼ tsp. granulated sugar
1/3 cup mayonnaise (homemade is best)
sliced white or whole wheat bread

Using the large canister of your Bravetti Do-It-All II, chop the olives until fine. Add the eggs and pulse until coarsely chopped. Remove chopping blade and blade holder. Add the spices and the mayonnaise and mix gently with a fork.

Spread the mixture onto the bread, trim the crust and cut into rectangles. Decoratively arrange on a platter.

Note: This will make about 8 rectangle sandwiches so adjust the recipe as needed to accommodate desired yield.

> **Food Styling Tip** *To make sandwiches for entertaining, spread the egg salad lightly on a slice of whole wheat bread and top with a slice of white bread. Turn half of the sandwiches over so there are equal number of wheat and white topped. Trim the crust and slice the bread in half lengthwise and then half width wise to form small squares. Slide a toothpick through a small grape tomato and into the center of each square. Arrange the rectangles on a platter.*

Salads
&
Dressings

A scrumptious salad day or night,
Treats your palette oh-so-right!

Tropical Chicken Salad

When I first made this recipe on HSN, I never dreamed how popular it would become! All of the show hosts and crew eat it after the show...even at 6 am! It is absolutely delicious and makes a beautiful presentation if you opt for the serving suggestion below!

2 cans breast of chicken; well drained
1 small can mandarin oranges; well drained
1 small can pineapple tidbits; well drained
½ cup shredded coconut
½ cup sliced almonds
½ cup chopped celery
½ cup mayonnaise
½ tsp. Salt
½ tsp. Ground black pepper
1 whole pineapple, optional serving suggestion below

Using the traditional beaters of your Hand Mixer and mix all ingredients together on medium speed until chicken is shredded and all ingredients are well blended.

Serve on a bed of lettuce as a salad or with crackers for a refreshing dip.

Food Styling Tip:

Use a very sharp knife to lengthwise cut the top off of a whole pineapple leaving the leaves intact. Hollow out the inside of the pineapple and dry with paper towels. Scoop the chicken salad into the pineapple. Place the pineapple onto a serving platter and arrange crackers and celery stalks around it.

Shrimp Salad

I love to order this out for a light lunch, but it is so expensive! I can make 4 servings at home for the same price and my friends all think I'm a big spender!

1 lb. frozen baby salad shrimp; thawed under cool running water and patted dry
½ cup thinly sliced celery
¼ cup chopped green onions
3 eggs; hard boiled, peeled and chopped
½ cup sweet pickles; chopped
1 cup mayonnaise
½ cup cultured sour cream
½ tsp. salt
¼ tsp. pepper

Place all ingredients together into a medium glass bowl. Toss lightly until well mixed. Cover and refrigerate at least 1 hour. Serve on a bed of lettuce with ripe tomato wedges.

Food Styling Tip:

This looks beautiful when served in a hollowed avocado shell. Save out a little of the chopped egg and sliced celery to sprinkle on the top of the individual servings!

Farmhouse Salad

Nothing fancy, but great for a family get together or to pack in a cooler for a picnic!

For Salad:
1 head iceberg lettuce; washed, cored and torn into bite-size pieces
2 medium tomatoes; seeded and chopped into large pieces
1 medium cucumber; peeled and medium-thin sliced
1 large carrot; peeled and sliced into thin rounds
1 large stalk celery; thinly sliced
1 small red onion; peeled and sliced into thin rounds
6 radishes; root trimmed and thin sliced
Seasoned Croutons

For Farmhouse Dressing:
1 cup mayonnaise
½ cup sour cream
½ teaspoon dry mustard
¼ teaspoon salt
2 teaspoons sugar
2 teaspoons vinegar
¼ teaspoon coarse ground black pepper
2 tablespoons milk; use a little more for desired consistency.

Wash and prepare all the vegetables and place into a large salad bowl.

Combine all dressing ingredients together in a small bowl or blender adding additional milk until you reach your desired consistency.

Pour dressing over vegetables and toss to coat thoroughly. Cover and refrigerate until ready to serve. Toss again and top with seasoned croutons.

Three Bean Salad

I used to buy this until I found out how easy it is to make. Now I always have some in my fridge! It makes a good side dish to sandwiches and is a great addition to your anti pasta tray.

1 can red kidney beans; drained and washed
1 can long yellow (or wax) beans; drained
1 can long green beans; drained
1 medium onion; chopped
¾ cup sugar
1 teaspoon salt
½ teaspoon black pepper
1/3 cup salad oil
2/3 cup vinegar

Heat on low, in a medium saucepan, the onion, sugar, salt, pepper, oil and vinegar.

Put prepared beans into a medium glass bowl. Pour heated mixture over beans. Toss and refrigerate for at least 24 hours before serving. This salad will keep in the refrigerator for several days.

English Pea Salad

This Southern-Born salad is so basic, but so good! I took it over to my friend Debra Murray's house one night and she loved it. That's a huge compliment as Deb is one of the best cooks I've ever known, on and off HSN! It just goes to show that simple things are often the best things.

2 cans English peas; drained
½ lb. sharp cheddar cheese; cut into small cubes
2 hard boiled eggs; finely chopped
2/3 cup mayonnaise
2 tablespoons milk
1 tablespoon sweet pickle juice
½ teaspoon salt
¼ teaspoon black pepper

In a small-medium serving bowl, place the peas, cheese cubes and chopped egg. In a large measuring cup mix together the remaining ingredients; pour over pea mixture. Use a fork to toss the ingredients together being careful not to mash the peas.

Cover and refrigerate until ready to serve.

Spinach Salad with Hot Bacon Dressing

I think this is almost as good as my Mom makes it! This is one salad that I can eat as my whole meal and feel completely satisfied.

6 oz. fresh tender spinach
3 strips bacon; cooked and crumbled
2 Tbsp. warm bacon drippings
2 Tbsp. olive oil
4 Tbsp. wine vinegar
½ tsp. dry mustard
3 dashes soy sauce
¼ tsp seasoned salt
½ cup fresh sliced mushrooms
¼ cup thinly sliced red onion
2 hard boiled eggs, peeled and chopped
garlic croutons

Wash and dry spinach leaves; remove stems and cut into but sized pieces. Heat skillet. Cook bacon to crisp, remove and drain on paper towel. Discard all but 2 Tbsp. bacon drippings from the skillet. Add to the drippings, the olive oil, vinegar, soy sauce and salt.

When dressing is thoroughly heated, add bacon, mushrooms and onion; toss and remove from heat. Add the spinach leaves tossing quickly to just cover leaves with dressing.

Place salad into a salad bowl, or on individual plates, and top with chopped egg and croutons.

Party Pasta Salad

This tasty recipe makes enough for a small army so cut it back if you don't have many mouths to feed! It also looks great on your table.

16 ounces mini penne pasta
1 pint grape tomatoes; or halved cherry tomatoes
½ cup chopped cucumber
2 2 1/2 oz. cans sliced black olives
½ cup broccoli florets; broken into small pieces
1 8 oz. jar marinated mushrooms; drained
¼ cup sliced green onions
1 cup diced provolone cheese
1 cup diced hard salami
1/3 cup extra light olive oil
½ cup red wine vinegar
2 Tbs. Dijon mustard
2 tsp. dried basil
1 tsp. dried oregano
½ tsp. dried thyme
2 Tbs. dried parsley
½ tsp. salt

Cook pasta according to package directions. Run under cold water and drain well. In a large bowl, combine pasta, tomatoes, cucumber, olives, broccoli, mushrooms, onions, and salami; mix gently.

In small bowl, whisk together the oil, vinegar, mustard and spices. Pour over pasta mixture; toss gently. Cover and refrigerate at least 2 hours. Add cheese and mix gently before serving.

Food Styling Tip

Whenever you are making a salad or dish with many ingredients that need slicing, try to cut them all about the same size! For example, in this salad, you use grape tomatoes. Use these as a guideline size for cutting the broccoli, cheese and cucumbers!

Waldorf Salad

Simple, elegant and delicious! You can't go wrong serving this!

1 cup celery; diced
1 cup apples; diced
1 cup seedless red or green grapes; halved
½ cup walnuts; chopped
¾ cup mayonnaise, homemade or store bought

Toss all ingredients together. Chill and serve.

Holiday Fruit Salad

This is one of my family's favorites! Especially the next day when I serve the leftovers as a dessert by spooning some over a slice of pound cake!

1 cup coconut; shredded
1 cup Mandarin oranges; canned, drained
1 cup pineapple bits; canned, drained
1 cup sliced pears; canned, drained
1 cup sliced peaches; canned, drained
½ cup Maraschino cherries; drained
1 cup walnuts; coarsely chopped
½ cup sour cream
1 cup miniature marshmallows

Mix all ingredients together in a large glass bowl. Cover and let set overnight.

Food Styling Tip

When making fruit salads, choose the best-looking and firmest fruits! If using canned, buy the more expensive brands, as they tend to use better fruits. Also, do not over-stir the salads; toss the ingredients together gently! When adding nuts, use only the coarsely chopped pieces as the very small, particles will give the salad a brownish color.

Hot German-Style Potato Salad

I love to serve this salad with a thick Rueben sandwich on a cold day! If my Brother John is around, I always have to make double because he likes it so much!

6 medium sized all-purpose potatoes
4 strips bacon
¼ cup onion; chopped
1 dill pickle; chopped
¼ cup water
½ cup vinegar
½ teaspoon sugar
½ teaspoon salt
¼ teaspoon celery seed
¼ teaspoon dry mustard

Gently boil potatoes, with skins on, until tender. Peel and slice thin while still hot; set aside.

In medium skillet, cook bacon until crispy. Remove bacon from skillet, reserving drippings, and chop.

Add the chopped onion to the drippings in the pan and sauté until golden. Add the chopped bacon, the chopped pickle and the remaining ingredients and cook until hot and bubbly.

Toss in the potatoes until heated throughout. Serve hot.

Eggs Benedict with Home-Fried Potatoes (above)   Sour Cream Banana Nut Bread (below)

Antipasto Party Tray & Artichoke Spinach Dip

Baked French Onion Soup with Cesar Salad (above)   Tropical Chicken Salad (below)

Hoppin' John with Corn Bread

Dill Red Potato Salad

This salad is great cold, but is also delicious hot when served with a beef roast! The dill gives it a wonderful flavor and makes it a pretty salad to serve.

10-12 small red new potatoes
½ cup mayonnaise
1 cup sour cream
½ teaspoon salt
1 tablespoon fresh dill weed, or more to taste
¼ teaspoon black pepper
¼ teaspoon prepared horseradish

Wash and quarter the potatoes. Cook in lightly salted boiling water until just tender. Drain and put into a medium serving bowl.

In a small mixing bowl, mix the remaining ingredients together thoroughly. Toss the mixture into the still-hot potatoes; cover and refrigerate until cold. Serve.

To serve hot: Simply dollop the creamy topping on top of the hot potatoes, or pass around separately and let everyone top their own potatoes!

Iceberg Wedges with Thousand Island Dressing

This simple salad is good with just about any dish you prepare! It is one of my Father's favorites so Mom made it all the time as I was growing up! Now, I always make it on HSN when I am demonstrating a blender to show the chopping power and so that I have lunch afterward!

1 medium head firm iceberg lettuce
2 hardboiled eggs; chopped

Wash and core the lettuce being careful to keep it in a tight head. Remove loose outer leaves and discard.

Working lengthwise cut the lettuce in half and then half again, forming 4 wedges; you may cut it into six wedges if desired. Place each wedge on a salad plate and cover generously with Thousand Island dressing. Top with chopped egg.

Thousand Island Dressing:

¼ cup milk
1 cup mayonnaise
1/3 cup chili sauce
½ cup ketchup
juice of 1 small lime
4-6 medium sweet gherkin pickles

Use your Bravetti Blender or blender attachment of you Bravetti Prep Center.

Place the milk, mayonnaise, chili sauce, ketchup, limejuice and pickles together, in that order, into the blender. Pulse or blend on low until completely mixed and smooth, scraping down the sides if necessary.

Tomato, Mozzarella & Cucumber Salad with Balsamic Vinaigrette

This is my Husband Al's absolute favorite; he likes it with any meal! That's great with me because it is extremely easy to make!

2 medium tomatoes
1 medium cucumber
½ small red onion
8-ounces mozzarella

Cut into small wedges and remove most of the seeds and attached moist meat.

Peel the cucumber, slice in half lengthwise and thin into thin half-rounds.

Peel the onion and trim both ends. Slice very thin and then separate the rings, discarding the smallest rings toward the middle.

Cut the mozzarella cheese into small cubes about ½-inch square.

Place above ingredients into a glass bowl, toss with desired amount of chilled Balsamic Vinaigrette and serve immediately.

Balsamic Vinaigrette

¼ cup extra virgin olive oil
¼ cup vegetable oil
¼ cup good balsamic vinegar
½ teaspoon oregano leaves
½ teaspoon basil leaves
2 cloves garlic; minced
½ teaspoon salt

Combine all ingredients together in a blender until smooth and well mixed. Chill mixture.

Cole Slaw

A must have at any cookout or picnic! To me, the key to good Cole Slaw is to slice the cabbage very, very thin and to pick out any large or tough pieces of cabbage; that way the salad will be light with no overpowering cabbage taste!

1 medium head cabbage; cored and thinly shredded (about 6 cups packed)
1 cup carrots; finely chopped or shredded, rinsed and patted dry
1 cup mayonnaise (homemade or store-bought)
2 tablespoon milk
2 tablespoons sweet pickle juice
¼ teaspoon salt
1 lg. dash white pepper
½ teaspoon lemon juice
1 teaspoon sugar

Toss the prepared cabbage and carrots together in a large bowl. In a small bowl, mix together the remaining ingredients until well blended. Add to the cabbage and carrots and toss until cabbage is completely coated.

Refrigerate 2-3 hours or overnight and toss again before serving.

Mayonnaise

Basic mayonnaise is the base to many salad dressings. Try adding herbs, garlic, extra lemon or horseradish to spice it up!

1 egg
½ teaspoon lemon juice or white vinegar
1 cup good oil; vegetable or olive
½ teaspoon salt

Place the egg, lemon or vinegar, salt and 2 tablespoons of the oil into a large measuring cup. Use your immersion blender and whip until slightly thickened. Slowly drizzle in the remaining oil, while blending, until the mayonnaise is thick. Refrigerate.

Hint: You may also make this in a blender, drizzling the oil through the top opening while the blender is running.

● ●

Southern-Style Mustard Potato Salad

A good homemade potato salad is a great addition to any casual meal, picnic or cookout! It is very easy to make and tastes so much better than the store-bought tubs!

6-7 medium-large Yukon gold or all-purpose potatoes; about 4 pounds
3 eggs
1 teaspoon salt
3 celery stalks; finely chopped or sliced
¼ cup chopped dill pickle
1 cup miracle whip
½ teaspoon salt
2 tablespoons prepared yellow mustard
paprika

Peel potatoes and cut them into 1- 1 ½-inch cubes. Place the potatoes and three whole, raw eggs into a large Dutch oven. Fill the pot with cold water to cover 2-inches above potatoes. Add salt. Place over high heat, bring to a boil, reduce heat and boil gently 15 minutes or until potatoes are just fork tender.

Pour the potatoes and eggs into a colander; run cold water over all for 1-2 minutes. Remove eggs. Place potatoes into the refrigerator for 30 minutes to cool. Peel the eggs, chop 2 and save one to slice on the top of the finished potato salad.

When potatoes have cooled, gently mix together with the celery, dill pickle, miracle whip, salt and prepared mustard. The potatoes will not stay in cubes.

Slice the remaining egg and place atop finished potato salad; sprinkle with paprika.
Cover with plastic wrap and refrigerate at least 1 hour before serving.

Classic Cesar Salad with Creamy Cesar Dressing

This is the perfect accompaniment to any dish. Try tossing on grilled chicken or shrimp to make it a main meal!

1-2 large heads romaine lettuce; washed, dried and cut into 2-inch ribbons
¼ cup Parmesan cheese; finely shredded
1 cup garlic croutons

Creamy Cesar Dressing:

1 egg
1 ¼ cup olive oil
juice of 1 lemon
4-5 anchovy fillets
¼ teaspoon dry mustard
¼ teaspoon coarse ground black pepper
¼ cup milk

Prepare the lettuce and place in a large salad bowl. Sprinkle on the Parmesan cheese.

To make the dressing, place 1 raw egg, ¼ cup olive oil and the juice of 1 lemon into a blender or beaker (if using an immersion blender). Begin processing. Slowly drizzle in, in a slow stream, the remainder of the olive oil; the mixture should turn very thick and mayonnaise-like. Add the anchovies, mustard, pepper and milk and process until creamy. Add a little more milk to thin as desired.

It is best to refrigerate the dressing for an hour or so before tossing it with the lettuce. Top salad with croutons and serve.

Savory Soups

Clear or creamy,
Soups are dreamy!

Old-Fashioned Chicken Noodle Soup

This soup takes a little time, but is absolutely great! The secret lies in roasting the chicken rather than boiling; it make a richer broth!

3-4 lb. Whole Fryer Chicken
2 Tbsp. Olive Oil
1 Tbsp. Butter
1 Medium Onion; peeled and halved
2 whole celery stalks with leaves
2 whole carrots
1 cup water; plus more as needed
8 cups canned low-sodium chicken broth
1 ¼ cup chopped celery
1 ¼ cup chopped carrots
2 tsp. kosher salt
1 tsp. Ground black pepper
1 tsp. Thyme
1 Tbsp. Dried parsley
8 oz. wide egg noodles

Wash, pat dry, lightly salt and pepper chicken inside and out. Place chicken into a roasting pan with 1 cup water, 1 halved onion, 2 whole peeled carrots and 2 celery stalks. Roast, uncovered, in a 350° oven for 1 ½ - 2 hours or until chicken is done. Check the chicken every half-hour to make sure there is enough liquid in the pan; add more water as needed.

Remove chicken from oven. Transfer chicken to a cutting board; save the liquid and vegetables for later use. Remove the bones and skin from the chicken and discard. Cut the chicken meat into bite sized pieces and set aside.

Pour liquid and vegetables into a food processor and puree; pour into a large stockpot. Add the chicken broth, chopped vegetables and seasonings. Allow to come to a boil. Add chicken, return to a boil, cover and simmer for 30 minutes. Add the noodles and cook an additional 12 minutes or until noodles are tender. Serve immediately and refrigerate any leftovers.

● ●

Potato Leek Soup

I first had this soup sitting in a little Bistro in London with my Mom. It took me three tries to get it right at home, but I'm glad I kept at because it has become one of my favorites!

½ stick butter
1 large leek; green tops removed
8 medium white potatoes, peeled and quartered
4 cups chicken broth
1 cups water
1 tsp. Salt
½ tsp. Ground black pepper
½ cup heavy cream

Thinly slice the white only of the leek; you should end up with about 1-1 ¼ cups. Heat butter over medium heat in a 6 qt. pot. Gently sauté leeks until tender but not browned. Add chicken broth, water, potatoes, salt and pepper. Bring to boil, reduce heat and simmer covered over medium-low heat for 20 minutes. Uncover, increase heat until a gentle boil is achieved and continue cooking for another 20 minutes. Remove from heat and allow to cool for 10 minutes.

Using an Immersion Blender or Food Processor, process potatoes and leeks until completely smooth. Return processed mixture to your pot over medium-low heat; add cream and heat until mixture is warmed throughout. Do not boil!

Serve with Caesar Salad and Garlic Croutons, if desired.

Food Styling Tip

Whenever you are serving a cream soup, especially one that is mainly 1 color, save a little of the raw ingredients, or use a compatible spice to sprinkle on top of the soup for serving. For example, this soup would look pretty with some finely shredded leek leaves on top!

Great Northern Bean Soup

Don't you just love the hearty flavor of a good bean soup on a cold day? I sure do!

16 oz. dried great northern beans
10 cups water
2 Tbs. Oil
8 oz. ham cubes
1 small onion, chopped fine
7 cups water
1 cup celery ribs and leaves, sliced
1 cup carrots, chopped
2 bay leaves
1 tsp. Coarse ground black pepper
2 tsp. Kosher salt
3 dashes Tabasco
1 cup instant mashed potato flakes

Soak beans in cold water over night; or bring to a rapid boil, cover, remove from heat and let sit 1 hour. Drain and rinse beans.

Heat oil in a 6-8 quart stockpot over medium heat. Add ham cubes and brown lightly for about 1 minute. Add the onion and gently sauté another minute. Add the water and scrape the bottom of the pan with a spatula to loosen any ham bits. Add the rinsed beans and the remaining ingredients, except for potato flakes, replace lid and simmer over medium-low heat for 30 minutes. Check to make sure that the beans are tender; if not, replace lid and cook another 10 minutes. When beans are tender, stir in the potato flakes. Cover and allow to cook and thicken on low 5 minutes. If a thicker soup is desired, use ½ cup more potato flakes.

Cream of Mushroom Soup

It's the tarragon that gives this soup a great flavor! Don't omit it!

4 Tbsp. Butter
2 shallots; finely minced
1 lb. sliced mushrooms
1 tsp. salt
½ tsp. black pepper
1 tsp. tarragon flakes
¼ tsp. ground thyme
4 cups chicken broth
1 cup water
¼ cup heavy cream

In a large saucepan, melt butter over medium heat. Add shallots and mushrooms and cook gently 5 minutes, stirring frequently. Add salt, pepper, tarragon, thyme, chicken broth and water. Bring to a full boil and then reduce heat to medium. Cook uncovered 30 minutes. Remove from heat and allow to cool 10 minutes.

Using your Bravetti immersion blender or food processor, puree the mushrooms in the broth until it is as smooth as you desire.

Return to pot over low heat and stir in cream. Heat thoroughly but do not boil. Serve Immediately.

Food Styling Tip

Before I use the immersion blender to cream the soup, I ladle out about ¼ cup of the mushroom slices. Then when I go to serve the soup, I float a few slices on the top of each serving along with a leaf or two of tarragon!

Tomato Basil Soup

The basil really perks up the old-fashioned tomato soup I used to eat!

2 28-oz. cans whole peeled tomatoes
1 cup vegetable stock
1 tablespoon olive oil
2 cloves garlic; finely chopped
1 medium onion; chopped
¼ teaspoon dried thyme
½ cup fresh basil leaves; washed and sliced thin
pinch of sugar
salt and pepper to taste

Heat oil over medium heat in a 6 qt. Stock pot. Add garlic and onion and gently sauté about 1 minute. Add thyme and basil and sauté another minute. Add the tomatoes, water and a pinch of sugar. Bring to a full boil and cook 3 minutes. Cover, reduce heat and simmer for 30 minutes.

Use an immersion blender or food processor and puree.

Serve hot with garlic croutons (see index)!

Food Styling Tip

This soup would be nicely served by floating a crouton in the center and topping with a small whole basil leaf!

Collard Green Soup

A true Southern specialty! Try this in your home with hot cornbread and you'll be whistlin' Dixie!

4 slices thick-cut bacon
1 pound smoked ham steak with bone; cut into small cubes
1 small onion; chopped
8 cups water
1 large ham hock; about ¾ pound
1 bay leaf
½ teaspoon salt
1 15-oz. can small white beans
1 large baking potato; peeled and diced
2 16-oz. packages frozen collard greens; you may substitute turnip or mustard greens
3 turns of your pepper grinder set on very coarse

Take the greens out of the freezer and leave them, unopened, on the counter until ready to use.

Heat a 6 qt. Stainless steel stockpot over medium-high heat. When the pot is hot, add the bacon. Reduce heat to medium and cook bacon for 4 minutes, stirring often and being careful not to burn the bacon. Remove bacon and discard (or save for another use), leaving the drippings in the pot. Add chopped ham and onion to the drippings. Using a wooden spoon, stir constantly while scraping the bottom of the pan to loosen any stuck on bacon. Cook for 2 minutes.

Add the water, the ham bone, ham hock, bay leaf and salt. Bring to a full boil, cover, reduce heat to medium-low and cook at a low boil about 30 minutes. Add the beans, potatoes and turnip greens and pepper. Bring to a full boil and cook uncovered 10 minutes. Reduce heat, cover and continue cooking another 15 minutes or until potatoes and greens are tender.

Discard the bay leaf, ham hock and ham bone. Serve hot!

Florida Fish Chowder

Imagine yourself sitting dockside, watching the sunset over the Gulf of Mexico, while eating this steamy soup! Ummm, Heavenly!

1 cup diced potatoes
1 cup sliced carrots
½ cup diced celery
1 cup canned corn; drained
½ teaspoon salt
2 tablespoons butter
1 medium onion; thinly sliced
1 ½ - 2 pounds fresh grouper, snapper or other firm-meat fish; skinned and boned
1 teaspoon Worcestershire sauce
1 teaspoon salt
¼ teaspoon pepper
2 ½ cups milk
¼ cup water
2 teaspoons corn starch
paprika

Wash the fish well and cut into 1" pieces.

In a 6-qt. Stockpot, cover the potatoes, carrots, celery, corn and salt in water and cook over medium heat until the vegetables are almost tender; about 15-20 minutes.

In a separate saucepan, melt butter over medium heat. Add the onions and sauté gently until the onions are soft but not brown. Add in the fish and Worcestershire sauce and cook gently for just 1 minute.

Add the fish and onion mixture to the vegetables and cook for 10 minutes. Add the salt, pepper and milk and slowly bring mixture to a gentle boil. In a small bowl or cup, mix together the corn starch and ¼ cup water; pour into gently boiling fish mixture. Stir, remove from heat, and allow to sit for 5 minutes. Ladle into bowls and sprinkle with paprika.

Carrot Soup

This simple soup has a delicious, uncomplicated flavor that reminds us that the simple things in life are best. You can make it visually appealing by following the serving suggestion below.

4 tablespoons butter
1 medium onion; chopped
1 pound carrots; peeled and sliced
4 cups chicken stock or broth
salt
a pinch of cayenne pepper
½ cup sour cream
2 tablespoons chopped chives

Melt the butter over medium heat in a large saucepan. Stir in the onion and carrots, cover the pan and cook gently for 30 minutes stirring occasionally.

Pour in the stock, add a little salt, and bring the soup to a boil. Reduce the heat, cover and cook another 30 minutes.

Use an immersion blender or food processor and blend until smooth. Pour through a sieve and mash out as much liquid as you can and return to the pan over low heat until heated throughout.

Food Styling Tip

Ladle into soup bowls and top with a dollop of sour cream, a sprinkling of chives and a pinch of cayenne.

Vichyssoise

The first time I heard of "cold potato soup", I thought "yuck"! Boy was I wrong, this stuff is delicious, easy to make and really impresses guests!

4 large sweet yellow onion; thinly sliced
1 tablespoon butter
2 ½ cups diced potatoes
2 cups chicken stock
¼ teaspoon paprika
salt and white pepper to taste
2 cups milk
1 cup heavy cream
chopped chives

Melt the butter, in a large saucepan, over medium heat. Add the onions and cook until just tender; about 5 minutes. Add the potatoes and stock. Bring to a boil, cover, reduce heat and cook at a gentle boil for 25 minutes, stirring occasionally. Add the paprika, salt and pepper and continue cooking another 20 minutes.

Use an immersion blender or food processor and puree the mixture until completely smooth. Chill completely and then whisk in the milk and cream until completely incorporated.

Ladle into bowls and top with chopped chives.

Cream of Asparagus Soup

The best asparagus for soup are large stalks with closed tips. At the end of the season you can often find large quantities available at reasonable prices; that's a great time to try this recipe!

3 pounds fresh asparagus
2 tablespoons butter
1 small onion; chopped
6 cups chicken stock
salt and freshly ground black pepper to taste
½ cup whipping cream
2 tablespoons cornstarch blended with 2 tablespoons cold water
Parmesan cheese for garnish

Remove the woody ends of the asparagus and cut into 1-inch pieces.

Melt the butter in a large heavy saucepan over medium-high heat. Add the onion and asparagus and cook for about 6 minutes, stirring often. The asparagus should turn bright green, but not allowed to brown.

Stir in the stock and bring to a boil over high heat and skim off any foam that comes to the surface. Reduce heat to medium and simmer for 8 minutes or until the tips are tender. Using a slotted spoon, remove 12-14 tips for garnish; cover and set aside. Season the soup with salt and pepper, cover and continue to cook for 20 minutes or until stalks are very tender.

Use an immersion blender or food processor and puree until smooth. Return mixture to pot and bring to a boil over medium-high heat; stir in cream. Whisk the water and cornstarch mixture into the boiling soup and boil for 1-2 minutes until slightly thickened.

Ladle into bowls and top with reserved asparagus tips and shredded Parmesan cheese.

Tortilla Soup

This is the first course of a casual Mexican meal!

1 14.5-oz. can tomatoes
1 medium onion; chopped
1 clove garlic; chopped
2 tablespoons cilantro
¼ teaspoon sugar
salt and pepper
5 cups chicken broth
2 cups Monterey jack cheese; cut into small cubes
2 medium avocados; cubed
8 ounces corn tortilla chips; broken into bite-sized pieces
sour cream
chopped cilantro

In a food processor, blend undrained tomatoes, onion, garlic, cilantro and sugar together until chunky-smooth. Simmer tomato mixture with the chicken broth in a large saucepan over medium heat for 20 minutes. Taste and season with salt and pepper as desired.

To serve, place cubed cheese, avocado and tortilla chips in the bottom of the bowl and ladle in the hot soup. Top with sour cream and a sprinkling of cilantro. Serve immediately.

Food Styling Tip

Height adds an attractive dimension to any meal. Save a few taller pieces of tortilla chips and place them upright into the center of the sour cream on top of the soup. Also, add a sprig of cilantro along with the chopped!

Cheesy Chicken Soup

This is a great way to use leftover chicken and the whole family will love it!

4 tablespoons butter
¼ cup onion; chopped fine
½ cup sliced carrot
½ cup sliced celery
4 cups chicken stock
1 cup whipping cream
1 pound American processed cheese; diced
2 cups cooked chicken; chopped
salt and pepper to taste
chopped parsley for garnish

In a large saucepan, melt the butter over medium heat. Sauté the onion, carrot and celery for 10 minutes, stirring often. Add the chicken stock and simmer for 15 minutes of until vegetables are tender.

Add the cream and cook another 5 minutes. Add cheese and chicken and simmer until cheese melts, constantly stirring and scraping the bottom of the pan.

Season with salt and pepper and top with chopped parsley.

Vegetable Beef Soup

After smelling this cook all afternoon everyone is starving! Good thing it makes a lot!

2 pounds stew meat; cut into small pieces
2 tablespoons vegetable oil
8 tablespoons butter
1 cup flour
8 cups water
2 cups sliced carrots
1 ½ cups sliced celery
1 large onion; chopped
1 16-oz. package frozen mixed vegetables
1 16-oz. can chopped tomatoes
1 teaspoon Accent
4 tablespoon Kitchen Bouquet
3 teaspoons beef stock base
salt and pepper to taste

In a large skillet, brown beef well in oil, drain and set aside.

In a large stockpot, melt butter over medium-high heat and stir in flour stirring constantly. Very slowly add water, one cup at a time to prevent mixture from becoming lumpy.

Add carrots, celery, onion, frozen mixed vegetables and tomatoes. Add accent, Kitchen Bouquet, beef stock base, salt and pepper. Add browned meat, cover and simmer on medium-low for 2 hours, stirring occasionally. Uncover and cook another hour.

Serve with hot crusty French bread and a green salad.

Chili

Everyone has a favorite Chili recipe; this is mine! I like it thick, but not too thick, hot, but not too hot, with lots of beans! I always think Chili is better the next day so this is perfect to make ahead.

1 28-oz. can tomato puree
2 cups water
1 16-oz. can red kidney beans; drained
1 16-oz. can pinto beans; drained
2 teaspoons ground cumin
3 tablespoons chili powder
½ teaspoon salt
2 pounds coarsely ground lean beef
1 tablespoon vegetable oil
1 large onion; diced
½ green pepper; diced
1 clove garlic; chopped fine
3 tablespoons flour mixed with 3 tablespoons cold water
shredded cheddar cheese and sliced green onions for garnish

In a large stockpot, over medium heat, add the tomato puree, water, both cans beans, cumin, chili powder and salt.

In a large heavy skillet, brown the meat; drain and add to stockpot. Wipe skillet clean with a paper towel, add oil and heat over medium-high heat. Add onion, pepper and garlic, reduce heat to medium and sauté for about 5 minutes or until onions are tender. Add onion mixture to stockpot.

Bring mixture to a boil, cover, reduce heat and simmer for 2 hours stirring occasionally. Taste mixture, and adjust seasoning to your liking; adding more chili powder, cumin or salt if desired. Add more water if Chili gets too thick while cooking. Recover and cook another hour.

Slowly bring mixture to a gentle boil and add the flour water mixture. Cook to thicken another 5 minutes.

Ladle into bowls and top with shredded cheese and sliced green onions.

• •

Black Bean Soup

This is one of my very favorite soups! I love it over white rice and topped with chopped onions!

1 pound black beans

2 tablespoons olive oil
1 large yellow onion; chopped
½ green pepper; chopped
1 clove garlic; minced
8 cups water
1 large smoked ham hock
2 bay leaves
½ teaspoon salt
½ teaspoon cumin

Sort through the beans and pick out any small stones. Cover with cold water and soak overnight or bring to a rapid boil, cover, remove from heat and let sit for 1 hour.

Drain the beans, put into a large stockpot, cover with water and set over high heat. Bring to a boil and cook for 10 minutes. Drain, rinse well and set aside.

Heat the oil in the stockpot over medium-high heat. Add the onion, pepper and garlic, reduce heat to medium and sauté for 3-4 minutes until the onion is soft but not brown. Add the 8 cups of water, the ham hock, bay leaves, salt and cumin. Add the beans and bring to a boil. Cover, reduce heat and simmer 1 ½ - 2 ½ hours or until beans are tender.

Remove the ham hock and bay leaves; discard. Using a slotted spoon, scoop out 1 cup of beans and mash them. Return the mashed beans to the pot and stir well. Cook uncovered over medium heat another 15 minutes.

Serve alone or over cooked white rice; top with chopped onion.

Minestrone

A very thick soup that is a meal in itself. This is my own version using the ingredients I like. Feel free to modify it to your liking!

6 Italian Sausages, 1 ¼ to 1 ½ pounds
4 ounces salt pork
2 tablespoons olive oil
2 cloves garlic; chopped
1 medium onion; chopped
2 celery ribs; thickly sliced
1 carrot; thinly sliced
4 cups chicken stock or broth
4 cups water
1 14-oz. can Italian peeled tomatoes; drained and chopped
1 head escarole or cabbage; leaves cut into 3 inch pieces
1 15-oz. can Cannellini beans (white kidney beans)
1 cup elbow macaroni
salt and pepper
hot pepper flakes
grated Romano cheese

Prick sausages all over with a fork. Place sausages and salt pork in a saucepan with 2 quarts of water. Bring to a boil and cook for 5 minutes over medium heat; drain. Cut sausages into bite-sized pieces and dice the salt pork.

In a large stockpot, heat oil over medium heat. Add salt pork, garlic, onion, celery and carrots. Cook 5 minutes, or until onions are soft. Add stock, water, beans and tomatoes. Bring to a boil and add escarole and sausages. Cook 20 minutes or until vegetables are tender.

Add pasta and simmer 6 minutes or until pasta is barely done. Taste and season with salt and pepper if desired.

Serve in bowls passing hot pepper flakes and grated Romano cheese on the side.

Baked French Onion Soup
with Croutons

After years of trying to create the perfect French Onion soup, I think I've finally gotten it just right! The roasted beef really adds the extra punch of flavor. I hope you like it as much as I do!

1 loaf French bread; cut into 2-inch slices
6 tablespoons butter
1 clove garlic
2 teaspoons olive oil
¾-1 pound prime rib or T-Bone steak
2 tablespoons Worcestershire sauce
salt and pepper
½ cup water
2 very large Spanish or Vidalia onions, about 1 ½ pounds;
quartered and sliced ¼ " thick
3 tablespoons butter
1 tablespoon olive oil
2 tablespoons flour
7 ½ cups water
3 tablespoons Better-Than-Bullion Beef Base
1 round slice Provolone Cheese for each serving
Parmesan cheese; finely shredded

Heat oven to 400°. Use 2 teaspoons olive oil to coat the bottom of a cold, oven safe stainless steel skillet. Lightly salt and pepper both sides of the steak and place it into the skillet with the oil. Pour the Worcestershire sauce over the steak and ½ cup water around the steak. Place pan into the preheated oven and cook for 30 minutes.

Remove pan from oven and transfer steak to cutting board; trim the fat and bone from the meat. Place the pan, fat and bone, 4 cups water and remaining Worcestershire sauce on stove and boil over high heat 15 minutes scraping the bottom of the pan.

Meanwhile, melt 4 tablespoons butter and 1 tablespoon olive oil in stockpot over medium heat. Add sliced onions, reduce heat to medium-low and cook slow, stirring often for 15 minutes or until onions are translucent.

Chop the cooled steak into tiny pieces and add to the onion. Sprinkle flour over the meat and onions and mix thoroughly. Strain the liquid in the pan into the onions and add remaining water and the beef base. Bring to a boil, cover, reduce heat to medium-low and simmer for 15 minutes.

Garlic Croutons: Melt the butter with the garlic clove in a small saucepan over low heat and let sit for 5 minutes. Brush both sides of the sliced French bread with the butter and place into 250° oven for 15 minutes on each side. Remove from oven. When they have cooled, cut each one into 6 pieces.

To assemble and serve: Place 3-4 croutons into the bottom of each ovenproof soup crock. Ladle soup over croutons. Top with a slice of Provolone and a generous sprinkling of the shredded Parmesan cheese cheese. Place under broiler until cheeses begin to melt and brown.

See Photo.

Granddaddy's Swamp Cabbage

Every year my Grandfather, my Dad and various other men relations would head down to the Florida Everglades to deer hunt. While there, Granddaddy would always make sure he found a Cabbage Palm and removed the heart to cooked up his special recipe in celebration of the hunt. He would fix this over the fire, in a large cast iron pot and serve it with the fresh venison. That's how the Heart of Palm became Swamp Cabbage!

2 14-oz. cans of hearts of palm; drained (I use Vigo brand)
1 4-oz. piece of salt pork (white bacon); rind removed and thickly sliced
4 cups water
1 tablespoon salt
1 teaspoon coarse ground pepper
½ cup sugar
4 tablespoons butter
4 cups whole milk

Drain the hearts of palm and rinse well with running water. Trim any hard or toughened places from the hearts, if necessary, and chop into ½-inch rounds.

Heat stockpot over medium heat and add the sliced salt pork. Sauté, stirring constantly, until it becomes slightly translucent; about 2-3 minutes. Add the water, salt, pepper, sugar and the cabbage. Bring the mixture to a boil, stirring occasionally with a wooden spoon. Simmer, covered, over low heat for 20-25 minutes or until 10 minutes before serving.

Just before serving, use a slotted spoon and remove the salt pork. Add butter and simmer until melted and then stir in the milk. Taste the mixture and adjust the salt, pepper and sugar to taste. Allow the mixture to heat through.

Serve immediately with wedges of hot cornbread or hushpuppies.

Entrées

The entrée
Is the main event of the meal,
So make it with Heart,
With Love
And with Zeal!

Mediterranean Salmon

I first made this dish on HSN using my pressure cooker and boy does it taste great! However, if you don't have a pressure cooker, it is also wonderful on the grill by using the variation below!

1 pound salmon fillet, washed
1 halved lemon
1/2 teaspoon dried oregano
1/2 teaspoon dried parsley
1 medium tomato, seeded and chopped
8 small black olives, pitted and sliced
2 teaspoons capers
2 tablespoons white wine
1 1/2 cups water

Place the salmon on a large square of aluminum foil. Squeeze the lemon over the fillet and top with the next 6 ingredients. Pinch the foil together to form a tight packet that seals in the fish . Place onto the steamer basket of your Pressure Cooker.

Add the water to the bottom of the pressure cooker pot and heat over high heat until it starts to boil. Lower the steamer basket with the fish/foil packet onto the steamer rack. Attach the pressure lid, set to setting II, and bring to pressure. When pressure is reached, lower heat to medium-low and cook for 5-6 minutes depending on the thickness of the fillet and your preference of doneness.

Turn the pressure release valve to I until no steam escapes and then to 0. When all the pressure is released, remove lid. Carefully remove steamer basket and rack. Open foil and serve fish and asparagus with white rice.

Variation: Assemble the fish in the foil pack as directed in the first paragraph. Preheat your grill on high. Place the foil packet on the grill and immediately lower the heat to medium-low. Close the lid and cook for 7-8 minutes or more if your fish is very thick.

Sesame Crusted Teriyaki Tuna

I had something like this at a restaurant one time and I couldn't wait to try it at home. It is really tasty and surprisingly easy to make. You can even thin slice it and serve as an appetizer!

1 pound tuna steak, 1" thick, cut in half lengthwise
1 cup teriyaki sauce
1/4 cup sesame seeds, roasted
2 tablespoons olive oil
1 tablespoon butter
1 teaspoon flour
2 cups cooked rice

Soak tuna steaks in teriyaki sauce for 10 minutes, turning once. Spread half of the sesame seeds on a sheet of wax paper. Remove one steak from the teriyaki sauce and press onto seeds. Sprinkle more seeds on top of tuna, turn over and press. Continue until both sides are covered with the sesame seeds. Repeat with the second steak; do not discard the teriyaki sauce.

Preheat oil, in a stainless steel pan, over medium heat. Add both steaks, reduce heat to medium-low, cover and cook 1 minute. Carefully turn steak, recover and continue cooking 4 minutes for medium well. Remove steaks and place atop cooked rice on warmed plates.

Add butter to the pan. When melted, add the flour and mix to a paste. Slowly pour in the remaining teriyaki sauce, stir and scrape the bottom of the pan. When mixture begins to boil, remove from heat and continue stirring until mixture thickens slightly. Pour sauce over the tuna steaks. Serve immediately.

Southern-Style Crab Cakes

These are wonderful! You can also make them very small and serve as appetizers!

2 cups fine fresh bread crumbs
2 large eggs; well beaten
1 tablespoon Dijon mustard
1 teaspoon Worcestershire sauce
3 tablespoons fresh parsley leaves; finely chopped
½ cup green onions; finely chopped
1 teaspoon Old Bay seasoning
salt and pepper
1 pound cleaned lump crabmeat; drain if using canned
4 tablespoons vegetable oil
French Style Rémoulade, Tartar Sauce or Mayonnaise (see index for recipes)
Lemon wedges

In a large mixing bowl, combine 1 ½ cups of bread crumbs with the eggs, mustard, Worcestershire sauce, parsley, onions and Old Bay seasoning. Season with salt and lots of pepper. Blend well. Fold in the crabmeat being careful not to break up the lumps.

Divide the mixture into 8-10 portions and shape them in hamburger-like patties. Coat each patty in the remaining breadcrumbs. Refrigerate until ready to cook.

Heat 2 tablespoons of oil in a non-stick skillet over medium heat. Fry the patties, 4-5 at a time, for about 2-3 minutes per side, or until golden brown. Drain on paper towels and serve immediately with lemon wedges and one of the sauces listed above.

Food Styling Tip

Refrigerate the mixture for 20-30 minutes before you form the patties; they hold their shape better

---

Garlicky Shrimp

I think these taste best on the grill, but you can always put them under the broiler when you want the flavor but it isn't grilling weather!

1 ½ pounds jumbo shrimp; shelled and deveined
½ cup extra-virgin olive oil
½ teaspoon salt
¼ teaspoon pepper
½ teaspoon dried oregano leaves
2 garlic cloves; minced
lemon wedges

In a plastic zip-type bag, combine the oil, garlic and seasonings. Add the shrimp so that they are all coated and refrigerate for 2 hours turning the bag occasionally.

Skewer the shrimp, threading them length wise through the body so they won't spin around, so that they just barely touch each other. Preheat your grill to medium-high.

Place the shrimp skewers on the grill and cook quickly; you will know they are ready to turn when they release themselves from the grill, about 2-3 minutes per side. Brush additional marinade on the shrimp as you turn them. Cook until the shrimp are well-seared but still opaque on the inside. Do not overcook!

Serve with lemon wedges.

Broiler Variation: Marinade as directed above and them place them in a single layer in an oven-safe dish. Place under the broiler, about 3 inches from heat, for 6 minutes. Turn the shrimp, brush with additional marinade, and cook another 4-5 minutes or until they are well-seared but still opaque on the inside. Do not overcook!

Serving Suggestion: These are great on top of a Cesar Salad!

Swordfish with Orange-Basil Butter

The combination of the orange with the basil gives this meaty fish a great light flavor. I like to serve this with a rice pilaf and a green salad.

4 swordfish steaks; cut ¾-inch thick, about 6 oz. each
2 tablespoons extra-virgin olive oil
¾ cup plus 2 tablespoons orange juice; no pulp
¼ teaspoon pepper
¼ cup chopped fresh basil; or 1 tablespoon dried
¼ teaspoon salt
1 stick butter; softened
grated zest of 1 orange

Combine oil, ¾ cup orange juice, pepper and ¼ of the basil in a small glass bowl. Generously brush both sides of the fish with the mixture. Place the fish on a plate, cover with plastic wrap and refrigerate for 1 hour.

Preheat broiler. Lightly salt both sides of the fish. Broil 3-4 inches from the heat, turning and basting once, for 8-10 minutes or until lightly browned outside and just opaque inside.

In a small bowl, use your hand mixer and beat together the butter, remaining basil, orange zest and 2 tablespoons orange juice.

Serve the hot fish with the cold butter.

Variation: You may also grill this fish over medium-high heat for about 4 minutes per side, basting as you turn.

Food Styling Tip

Pack the butter mixture into a small bowl and refrigerate until firm. After you plate the fish on individual dishes, place a slice of orange on each. Use a melon baler to scoop a round of the prepared butter and center a ball on each orange slice!

Trout Russian Style

I often order this at a restaurant over in Tampa and it is very good. The funny thing is the restaurant is Spanish and this dish is Russian; go figure! Anyway, it's one of my favorites wherever it comes from!

6-8 trout fillets; bones and skin removed
½ teaspoon salt
¼ teaspoon white pepper
2 eggs; well beaten
¼ cup milk
1 ½ cup dried bread crumbs
2 tablespoons vegetable oil
1 stick butter; softened
2 eggs; hard boiled and chopped
1/3 cup fresh parsley; chopped fine
2 tablespoons chopped pimento
2 lemons; thinly sliced

Make a paste with the butter, chopped egg, parsley and pimento. Set aside.

Wash, pat dry and salt and pepper the fish. Mix the raw eggs with the milk and pour into a shallow dish. Spread the breadcrumbs on a plate or piece of waxed paper. Dip the fish into the egg mixture and then press into the breadcrumbs, gently coating both sides.

Heat oil in a large non-stick skillet over medium heat. Cook the fish fillets until golden brown, about 5-6 minutes on each side. Drain on paper towels.

Place 1 or 2 fillets on each plate and spread with the butter mixture.

Food Styling Tip

Place a few lemon slices on each fillet and top with extra chopped egg and parsley!

Paella

If you watch HSN, you have seen Paella. Almost everyone who demonstrates pressure cookers makes this beautiful saffron-color dish using their favorite recipe! However, I don't think it tastes as good in a pressure cooker as it does prepared the traditional Spanish way; made in a Paella pan or large heavy skillet.

Traditional Paella, which originated in Valencia, Spain, is wonderful and often contains their local ingredients like snails, rabbit and quail. Here is the basic recipe to which any other ingredients may be added. I must warn you, however, that Paella can be an expensive dish due to the meats, seafood and the saffron (saffron is the most expensive spice in the world), is involved to make correctly, makes a large quantity and is not good as leftovers. Therefore, I only make it when I have at least 6 people coming to dinner, then it is well worth it effort and expense! Otherwise, I order it out at Spanish restaurants!

For Stock:

4 ½ cups boiling water
4 cubes chicken bouillon
1/8 teaspoon saffron powder
3 teaspoons salt
¼ teaspoon pepper
½ teaspoon crushed red pepper flakes, or to taste

Dissolve the bouillon in the boiling water and then add the spices. Have this stock very hot and ready to pour over the rice.

Paella:

¾ pound medium shrimp; shelled and deveined
12 little neck clams; rinsed
¾ pound scallops
12 tablespoons olive oil
3 chicken thighs; boned and cut in half
3 chicken breasts; boned and cut in half
1 ½ medium onions; chopped
½ green pepper; chopped
1 clove garlic; crushed

2 cups long grain rice
¾ pound boneless pork loin; cut into cubes
5 ounces sliced pepperoni; cut into strips
1 small package frozen peas
1 4-oz. jar chopped pimento

Paella Directions:

Blanch the peas in lightly salted boiling water. Set aside.

In a large deep oven-safe skillet with 3 tablespoons hot olive oil, sauté the shrimp and scallops for 1-2 minutes. Remove from pan and set aside.

Wipe out pan and add 9 tablespoons oil and sauté chicken pieces gently over medium heat until browned on all sides. Remove chicken and drain.

Sprinkle the pork with salt and pepper and add to the pan. Sauté for 2-3 minutes. Add onions to pan and fry until translucent. Add the green pepper and sauté until soft. Add garlic and sauté for 2-3 minutes. Stir in rice and cook until grains are transparent.

Lay chicken pieces in bottom of the pan and arrange all the remaining meats and seafood in the pan. Pour the hot chicken stock evenly over all. Add in the peas and pimento and bring to a quick boil.

Place pan on the middle rack of your preheated 375° oven. Bake, uncovered, until the rice is absorbed and all the ingredients are cooked; about 25-35 minutes. Remove from oven and toss lightly to distribute the ingredients before serving.

Food Styling Tip

To keep the rice from getting over-browned at the edges, tent the pan with aluminum foil to shield the heat but still allow the moisture to escape.

Shrimp Creole

I love the taste of this spicy dish; it reminds me of visits to New Orleans!

½ cup flour
½ cup corn oil
1 cups onions; chopped
½ cup celery; chopped
¼ cup bell pepper; chopped
1 cloves garlic; chopped
1 14.5-oz. can diced tomatoes
1 small can tomato paste
1 ½ teaspoon salt
pinch red pepper flakes; more if a spicier dish is desired
¼ teaspoon black pepper
3 cups water
1 ½ pounds medium sized raw shrimp; peeled and deveined
1 tablespoon chopped parsley
1 tablespoon chopped green onion tops
cooked white rice

Make a roux by browning the flour in the oil over low heat. Add the onions, celery, pepper and garlic and cook until soft. Add tomatoes, tomato paste, salt and the red and black pepper. Mix well, cook for about 5 minutes and then add the 3 cups water. Let simmer for about 1 hour over medium-low heat.

Add the shrimp and cook for 15 minutes. Add parsley and onion tops 5 minutes before serving. Serve hot over fluffy white rice.

Crab and Shrimp Au Gratin

Everyone likes this creamy casserole-type dish; be ready to pass out the recipe!
Plus, it's easy to make because you can buy the shrimp already cooked and deveined at the seafood counter! You can also bake this in 4-6 individual au gratin dishes for a dinner party.

2 tablespoons butter
2 tablespoons flour
¼ teaspoon salt
1 cup milk
24 medium shrimp; cooked, deveined and split
3 6-oz. cans crabmeat
1 3-oz. can sliced mushrooms; drained
2 tablespoons sherry
1 tablespoon lemon juice
dash of Tabasco
¼ teaspoon Worcestershire sauce
½ cup sharp cheddar cheese; grated
1 cup soft breadcrumbs; torn into pieces
2 tablespoons melted butter

In a large 2 quart saucepan, melt butter over low heat. Blend in flour and salt. Increase heat to medium and add milk all at once. Cook quickly, stirring constantly until sauce thickens and bubbles. Remove from heat. Add in the shrimp, crab, mushrooms, sherry, lemon juice, Tabasco and Worcestershire sauce; mix well.

Pour mixture into a well greased 9 x 13-inch casserole. Sprinkle cheese evenly over the top. Combine the breadcrumbs with the melted butter and sprinkle over the cheese.

Bake at 375° for 40 minutes or until hot, bubbly and heated through.

Southern-Fried Fish

Every summer, my family had a huge fish fry. My Dad, Uncle and Grandfather would use cast nets to catch enough Mullet (a very bony fish native to Florida's West Coast) for 20 or more people. After they scaled, skinned and filleted the fish, they would fry them in cast iron skillets. We would all eat the fish with slaw, hushpuppies, baked beans and Granddaddy's Swamp Cabbage!

I now make my fish on HSN using my Bravetti Flash Fryer. Every time I do, I have fish-fry flash backs and feel reminiscent! I guess I'm just a Florida Cracker at heart!

6 ½-inch thick fish fillets; whatever is fresh in your area
1 cup milk
2 cups yellow corn meal
½ cup flour
1 ½ teaspoons salt
½ teaspoon paprika
1 teaspoon lemon pepper
¼ cup vegetable oil or shortening; more or less according to pan size

Wash and pat dry the fish. Place the fish in a zip-type plastic bag and pour in milk. Seal the bag and refrigerate 30 minutes.

In a large plastic bag, mix together the cornmeal, flour, salt, paprika and lemon pepper.

Remove 3 fillets from the milk and pat dry. Place in the bag with the cornmeal mixture and shake well to thoroughly coat. Let sit in the bag for 5 minutes.

Heat ¼-inch layer of oil in a large heavy skillet (preferably cast iron) over medium-high heat until it shimmers. Give the fillets a final shake in the bag and gently place, one at a time, into the hot oil. Immediately reduce heat to medium and cook until both sides are crisp and stiff; about 3-4 minutes per side. Remove from pan, drain on paper towels and repeat with remaining fillets.

To Deep Fry: Follow directions above but cook in a 375° deep fryer for 6-8 minutes!

● ●

Shrimp Curry

I never used to like curry; I couldn't even stand to smell it cooking. Now, it's a flavor I often crave and have even started making at home. If you are not crazy about curry, give this recipe a try; you just might be surprised how much you like it!

2 pounds medium shrimp; cooked and cleaned
2 tablespoons margarine
2 small onions; chopped
1 clove garlic; minced
2 tablespoons curry powder
½ teaspoon salt
1 8-oz. can tomato sauce
1 cup chicken broth
3 tablespoons lemon juice
½ cup light cream
cooked white rice

Clean and cook shrimp for 5 minutes in lightly salted, boiling water.

Melt margarine over medium heat in a large saucepan. Add onion and garlic and cook until tender. Stir in curry powder and salt. Add tomato sauce and chicken broth. Cook over low heat, stirring occasionally, for 30 minutes.

Add the shrimp and lemon juice, stirring thoroughly. Then add the cream. Slowly heat through. Serve over hot fluffy white rice.

Food Styling Tip

Mound the rice in the center of the plate and then form a well in the center. Add the shrimp mixture to the well and top with a sprig of parsley. Sprinkle fresh chopped parsley on the rice ring around the edge.

English Battered Fish

3 pounds fillets, shrimp, oysters or scallops (or a combination)
1 cup all-purpose flour
oil for frying

Take the fish fillets and moisten with water. Then lightly flour the fillets and set them on a wire rack to dry. When they are dry, dip one piece at a time into the batter described above and fry in a pan for 4 minutes per side or in your deep fryer at 385° for 7-8 minutes.

Remove from oil and drain on a paper towel.

English Fish Batter

If you want fish like they have in England, you must use this batter! But, the English aren't the only ones known for their fried fish! In Florida, we have a local fish, the light delicious Black Grouper, which makes a great sandwich when fried using this batter.

2/3 cup beer
1/3 cup lemon juice
1 egg
½ cup self-rising flour
salt and pepper to taste

Mix the beer (any brand), lemon juice and self-rising flour in a large mixing bowl with a wire whisk. Whip the mixture until completely mixed. Let stand at room temperature for 10 minutes before using.

Florida Grouper Sandwich

4 battered and fried grouper fillets
4 egg hamburger-style buns
4 slices American cheese
lettuce, tomato and sweet onion

Batter and fry grouper fillets as directed above. Then set the fillets atop a slice of American Cheese on the bottom half of the bun. Top with Tartar Sauce, lettuce, sliced tomato and a slice of sweet onion (optional). Put on the top bun and enjoy!

Salmon with
Gingered Balsamic Vinegar Sauce

It's the sauce that makes this dish so special and gourmet-tasting! Do not omit it or you'll be sorry!

4 salmon fillets, about 6 ounces each; skin in tact
¼ teaspoon salt
freshly ground black pepper
Gingered Balsamic Vinegar Sauce; see recipe index

Wash, pat dry and season the fillets with salt and pepper.

To Broil: Position a shallow broiler pan 6 inches away from the heat source and preheat broiler. Remove pan from oven, spray with non-stick cooking spray and arrange fillets, skin-side down, on the pan. Broil, just until opaque, 5-7 minutes, or until the fish will flake using the tip of a knife. Place on warm platter and pour sauce overall.

To Grill: Prepare grill to hot. Spray the grate with the non-stick cooking spray. Arrange fish skin-side down, on the grill grate, cover and grill about 5 minutes or until opaque, and the fish will flake using the tip of a knife. Place on warm platter and pour sauce overall.

Food Styling Tip

Before plating the salmon fillet, drizzle some of the sauce around the outer edge of the plate. Then place the salmon in the middle and drizzle the sauce lengthwise down the fillet. Add a wedge of lemon and chopped fresh parsley to the center of the fillet.
Note, the salmon will be more attractive if it is grilled!

Southern Deep-Fried Chicken

I was never able to make good fried chicken until I started using the Bravetti Flash Fryer. Now I make it on HSN when I demonstrate the fryer because it comes out perfectly every single time! It's not fancy, but it sure is good...hot or cold! Just ask my son, Max, he adores it and I get a lot of pleasure from his enjoyment!

3 lbs. Chicken pieces; bone-in
8 cups cool water
2 Tablespoons salt
1 ½ cups flour
2 teaspoons salt
1 teaspoon paprika
½ teaspoon ground black pepper

Wash chicken and place into 8 cups water with 2 Tablespoons salt. Allow to soak for 30 minutes. Drain water and pat chicken dry.

Preheat your Deep Fryer to 375°.

Place flour and seasonings into a large zip-close baggie. Add chicken, 2-3 pieces at a time, to baggie and toss to thoroughly coat chicken pieces. Allow to sit 5 minutes and then toss again.

When fryer temperature indicator light goes out, remove lid and lower basket. Using long tongs, gently place chicken, one piece at a time, into the oil. Do not overcrowd the fryer. You may have to cook the chicken in two batches.

Cover fryer and cook for 13-15 minutes or until done. Raise lid and allow draining 30 seconds. Place chicken onto paper towel to remove any excess oils. Repeat with remaining chicken.

Hint: If you will be cooking several batches of chicken, place the cooked chicken in an oven-safe dish and keep warm, uncovered, in a 225° oven until all chicken is ready to serve.

Chicken Breasts with Artichokes, Cream and Tomatoes

I just love to make, and eat, this flavorful dish! It tastes like something I would order at an upscale restaurant!

6 chicken breasts; boneless, skinless
1 ½ tsp. salt
½ tsp. pepper
2 Tbsp. olive oil
1 Tbsp. butter
1 small onion, finely chopped
1 cup dry white wine
1 cup chicken broth
1 Tbsp. granulated chicken bouillon
1 14 ½ oz. can diced tomatoes, drained
1 10 oz. can artichoke hearts; drained and quartered lengthwise
1 ½ cups heavy cream
2 Tbsp. chopped fresh basil

Rinse chicken and pat dry. Season with half of the salt and pepper called for. In a large frying pan, heat oil and butter over medium-high heat. Add chicken and cook 3 to 4 minutes on each side or until lightly browned. Add onion, wine, chicken broth and bouillon to pan. Cover and simmer 25 minutes.

Remove chicken from pan. Boil pan juices until just ½ cup remains; about 3 top 5 minutes. Add drained tomatoes and artichokes to pan; cook for 1 minute. Add cream and basil; simmer slowly for 8 minutes or until just about 2 cups liquid remains. Season the pan with the remaining salt and pepper. Return chicken to pan and heat together for about 5 minutes, or until you a ready to serve; not longer than 10 minutes.

Serve over hot pasta and top with Parmesan cheese, if desired.

Chicken & Vegetable Risotto

Use a pressure cooker to make this delicious hearty feel-good dish! I make it on HSN every time I present the pressure cooker!

3-4 lb. Whole Fryer Chicken
2 Tbsp. Olive Oil
1 Tbsp. Butter
1 Medium Onion (coarsely chopped)
6 cups canned chicken broth
1 ¼ cup chopped celery
1 ¼ cup chopped carrots
½ lb. Sliced mushrooms
¼ cup chopped parsley
2 tsp. kosher salt
1 tsp. Ground black pepper
1 ¾ cup risotto
¾ cup Parmesan cheese

Heat olive oil and butter over medium heat in your pressure cooker; add onion and lightly brown. Add chicken broth. Wash, pat dry, and lightly salt and pepper the chicken inside and out and place into the broth and onions.

Cook under pressure for 45 minutes. Remove from heat, slowly release pressure and remove lid. Transfer chicken to a cutting board and allow the chicken to cool enough to handle. Remove the bones and skin from the chicken and discard.

Strain the liquid through a sieve. Discard the trappings and return the liquid to the pot. Cut chicken into bite size pieces and return to the broth. Allow the mixture to come to a gentle boil, add the rest of the ingredients and stir. Replace pressure lid, bring to pressure, over medium high heat, to the highest setting (III), and reduce heat to medium and cook for 7 minutes. Remove pan from heat and let stand 10 minutes. Release pressure, remove lid, stir gently with fork, replace lid and allow to rest another 5 minutes before serving.

Chicken Parmesan with Angel Hair Pasta

When I first started dating Al, my husband, he made this dish for me. I thought, "Wow, this guy can cook!" I always look forward to him making it because it is absolutely wonderful plus, I get the night off!

1 pound chicken scaloppini (or boneless, skinless chicken breast cutlets, pounded thin)
salt and pepper
2 cups dried seasoned breadcrumbs (he uses 4 C's brand)
2 eggs; well beaten
¼ cup milk
4 tablespoons olive oil
½ pound fresh mozzarella cheese; shredded
3 cups marinara sauce; homemade or from a jar
½ pound cooked angel hair pasta

Wash, pat dry and lightly salt and pepper the chicken. Beat the eggs well with the milk. Place the breadcrumbs on a plate or waxed paper.

Heat the oil over medium heat in a large skillet until hot. Dip the chicken, one piece at a time, into the egg mixture and then press into the breadcrumbs coating on both sides evenly.

Without overcrowding the pan, fry the coated chicken in batches, turning once until chicken is golden brown; about 3-4 minutes per side. Remove from pan and drain on paper towels. Cover the top of the chicken with another paper towel and gently press to remove any excess oil on the top of the chicken.

Place the chicken, in a single layer, onto a cookie sheet. Ladle about enough marinara sauce onto each piece of chicken to lightly cover the top surface. Sprinkle with shredded mozzarella cheese. Place pan of chicken into a 325° oven and cook until cheese is completely melted and beginning to brown.

Serve with hot angle hair pasta and remaining marinara sauce. Top with Parmesan cheese if desired.

Vertical-Roasted Chicken

This recipe makes the juiciest, best-tasting chicken you'll ever eat! To get the best results however, you must use the same vertical roaster used in famous restaurants worldwide...the Spanek Vertical Roaster! Once you've eaten chicken (or turkey for that matter) cooked on this roaster, nothing else will do! I should know, I have cooked hundreds of these chickens for Mr. Spanek's cooking demonstrations at HSN and in London and Germany!

1 2-6 pound chicken
rotisserie seasoning (or Spanek Magic Seasoning)
1 Spanek Vertical Roaster

Preheat oven to 450°.

Wash and pat dry the chicken. Sprinkle the chicken generously with the seasoning and rub in. Place the chicken onto the roaster, neck up, and push down until the roaster comes through the neck cavity. Place chicken in a large shallow roasting pan. Add ½ cup water to the bottom of the pan; this prevents splattering.

Place the pan into the oven and cook for 15 minutes. Reduce heat to 350° and continue cooking 15-18 minutes per pound. If the chicken becomes too brown on the top, tear a hole in the middle of a piece of aluminum foil and slip over the ring so that the ring is open to the oven, but the top part of the chicken is covered.

When the chicken is done, remove from oven. Allow to sit 5 minutes and then slide a fork under the top ring of the roaster and transfer to a carving board or platter. Carve and enjoy!

Variations: Beginning at the neck of the chicken, gently separate the skin from the meat with your fingertips forming a pocket over the breast area. Stuff into the pockets your choice of:

¾ cup mushrooms	½ cup onions	½ cup peppers
2 tablespoons fresh herbs	1 sliced lemon	½ cup salsa
2 tablespoons blue cheese	½ cup duck sauce	½ cup sliced fruit

For more information or to order a Spanek Vertical Roaster, visit www.spanek.com or call 1-800-446-3060

● ●

Lemon-Garlic Chicken Barbeque

A great tasting barbeque when you are tired of the red sauce!

1 cup vegetable oil
¾ cup lemon juice
3 teaspoons salt
1 teaspoon dried oregano
2 cloves garlic; peeled
1/2 teaspoon crushed red pepper
3-4 pounds chicken pieces

Combine the oil, lemon juice, salt, oregano, garlic and red pepper in a blender; process until smooth.

Place the chicken in a large glass dish. Pour the marinade over the chicken and toss well. Cover and refrigerate at least 6 hours; overnight is best.

Pour off the liquid, reserving it for basting.

Preheat your grill, or prepare your charcoals. Grill the chicken over medium until tender. Turn and baste often with the reserved marinade.

Note: Because the marinade has soaked with the raw chicken it is suitable only as a marinade to use while cooking. Discard any remains.

Food Styling Tip

Serve this dish on a large, dark colored platter and tuck lemon wedges about!

Easy Chicken Pot Pie

I love this dish anytime of year, but for some reason it reminds me of fall. Hearty and warm, but still a little light!

3 cups frozen peas and carrots
½ cup butter
½ cup flour
1 teaspoon salt
¼ teaspoon ground black pepper
½ teaspoon poultry seasoning
2 cups chicken broth
½ cup milk
1 10.5-oz. can cream of potato soup
1 3-oz can sliced mushrooms
4 cups cooked chopped chicken
2 Pillsbury unfold and bake piecrusts

Cook the peas and carrot as directed on package, drain and set aside.

Melt the butter in a saucepan over medium heat. Add in the flour, salt, pepper and poultry seasoning and stir, making a paste, for about 1 minute. Slowly stir in the chicken broth, milk and finally the soup. Bring mixture to a gentle boil, stirring often until is thick and bubbly. Add in the mushrooms and the peas and carrots; stir until well blended. Add the chicken and stir well.

Lightly grease the bottom and sides of a round 2 quart casserole and line with one of the crusts. Pour chicken mixture into the dish and top with the other crust. Pinch the edges of the 2 crusts together to make a seal. Use a sharp knife and make 3 small slits in the top crust.

Bake in a 400° oven for 40 minutes or until top is golden brown. Allow to sit for 5-10 minutes before serving.

Chicken and Yellow Rice Dinner

This yummy dish tastes like it cooked a long time but is surprisingly quick! It is colorful and tasty...just what I look for in demonstrations and for at-home!

2 pounds chicken pieces, washed and patted dry
4 - 6 tablespoons vegetable oil
3 tablespoons olive oil
½ cup onion, finely chopped
2 cloves garlic, finely minced
1 teaspoon salt
1 14 ½-oz. can diced tomatoes
1 bay leaf
2 1/3 cups hot water
1 cup chicken broth
1 pound yellow rice dinner (I use Vigo brand)
1 cup frozen baby peas (optional)

Heat, over medium, enough olive oil to just coat the bottom of a large deep skillet. Working in batches, cook the chicken for about 5 minutes on each side or until golden brown. Drain on paper towels.

Wipe out pan and heat 3 tablespoons olive oil. Sauté onions and garlic until tender. Add the salt and tomatoes; stir. Add the water, broth and bay leaf. Bring to a boil.

Add the rice and stir well. Place the chicken in the pan and sprinkle the peas on top. Bring the entire mixture to a boil, cover, reduce heat and cook 20-25 minutes or until the liquid is absorbed.

Variation: You can use boneless chicken if you prefer, but you may want to add a cube or two of chicken bouillon to compensate for the loss of flavor.

Chicken Enchiladas

Awhile back, I had the pleasure of living in Ft. Worth, Texas for 4 years. I really got hooked on the Tex-Mex and it just isn't the same anywhere else...unless you make it yourself using this recipe!

2 whole chicken breasts
water
½ small onion
1 bay leaf
8 peppercorns
½ teaspoon salt
½ medium onion; chopped
1 cup Monterey Jack cheese; shredded
1 cup Sharp Cheddar cheese; shredded
1 4-oz. can chopped green chilies
1 13-oz. can tomatillos, drained or use 1 ¾ cup drained canned tomatoes
¼ cup cilantro leaves
¾ cup whipping cream
1 egg
¼ teaspoon salt
1 cup water
8 flour tortillas
Guacamole (see index for recipe)
1 cup sour cream
2 cups shredded lettuce
12 black olives; pitted and sliced

Place the chicken breasts in a large pot with the water, onion, bay leaf, peppercorn and salt. Bring to a boil, reduce heat and simmer, covered, for 45 minutes. Remove chicken and shred; discard liquid. Mix the chicken with half of the cheeses and the salt; set aside.

Blend in a blender or food processor until smooth, the green chilies, tomatillos or tomatoes, cilantro, salt, whipping cream and egg. Set aside.

Preheat oven to 350°. Lightly grease the bottom of a 12 x 7 ½ -inch baking dish.

In a large skillet, heat water to boiling. Using tongs, quickly dip one tortilla at a time into the water to soften and lay it on a paper towel.

Place 1/8 of the chicken mixture onto the tortilla, roll tightly and place seam-side down in the baking dish. Repeat this process for the remaining 7 tortillas. Pour the chili-cream mixture over the enchiladas and sprinkle the remaining cheese evenly on top. Bake for 20 minutes or until bubbly and heated throughout.

Food Styling Tip

To serve beautifully, lightly cover the bottom and edge of individual plates with thinly shredded lettuce. Place two enchiladas on the plate and top each with about 3 tablespoons sour cream; lightly spread into a 3-inch circle. Add a dollop of guacamole to the center of the sour cream. Sprinkle finely chopped tomatoes and black olive slices across the center both enchiladas and around the plate atop the lettuce.

Cornish Game Hens

Whenever I want to have a romantic dinner at home, I serve these. They are delicious and easy to make but a little messy to eat because you have to use your fingers to get the tinier pieces of meat off the bone. Of course you can always lick each other's fingers!

2 Cornish game hen
1 tart apple; peeled cored and diced
¼ cup walnuts; chopped
1 slice bread; torn into little pieces
¼ cup brown sugar
½ cup consommé
2 slices bacon
½ cup sour cream
½ cup port
Kitchen Bouquet for color

Preheat oven to 400°.

Wash, pat dry and lightly salt and pepper the hens inside and out.

In a small bowl toss together the apple, nuts, bread and brown sugar; stuff into the cavity of the hens. Place the hens in a shallow roasting pan. Cut each slice of bacon in half and drape, forming an x, on top of each hen. Pour the consume and port in the pan, around the birds. Place in oven and bake, uncovered 40 minutes or until done; baste several times with the liquid in the pan.

Discard the bacon and arrange the birds on a warm platter. Place the roasting pan on the stovetop over medium heat and scrape the bottom. Slowly stir in the sour cream and a little Kitchen Bouquet. If the sauce is too thick, use a little water or consume to thin. Pour over and around the hens.

Serve with wild rice.

Quail in Wine Sauce

My Grandfather and Dad used to hunt for quail and my Grandmother would fry them in bacon drippings. Now days I have to pay for my quail at the grocer, so I prepare it a little more eloquently!

6 quail
1 stick butter
½ small onion; chopped
1 clove garlic
¾ cup celery; chopped
½ cup boiling water
salt and pepper
1 cup sauterne or dry white wine
1 cup heavy cream
3 cups cooked wild rice

Wash, pat dry and lightly salt and pepper the quail.

Melt the butter in a heavy skillet with deep sides. Sauté the birds with the onion, garlic and celery until the birds are brown. Add the boiling water. Cover and cook over low heat for 30 minutes. Add the wine and 1 teaspoon salt. Simmer uncovered until the birds are tender. Add more wine and salt to taste. Place the birds on a warm platter.

Strain the sauce and return it to the pan. Add 1 cup heavy cream and heat through but do not boil.

To serve, mound ½ cup wild rice in the center of a plate and place a quail on top. Drizzle the sauce around the rice and spoon a little on top of the bird.

Remember, quails are very small so if you are serving hungry people, plan for 2 per person!

Roast Duck with Cherry Rum Sauce

I learned to make this from a restaurateur who sat next to me on a flight to New York. I forgot his name, but I never forgot how to make this delicious dish!

2 cleaned ducks
salt and pepper
2 small onions
2 cloves garlic
1 bunch celery leaves
1/2 cup butter
1 cup boiling water
4 tablespoons butter
2 tablespoons flour
2 tablespoons dark rum
1 can tart whole, pitted cherries in heavy syrup

Preheat oven to 450°.

Scrub the ducks well, inside and out. Pat dry and lightly salt and pepper them.
Cut the tops off and peel the onions. Cut an x into the top and insert a clove of garlic. Divide the celery leaves and put half inside each duck, along with the onion.

Place the ducks, breasts up into a roasting pan. Melt the butter in the boiling water and pour around ducks in pan. Roast in oven 30 minutes, basting with the liquid in the pan at least three times. Add more water to the pan as needed. Caution: If the water in the pan dries up, you will have a lot of smoke in your house!

Remove the duck, slice thinly and put on a plate over boiling water to keep warm until serving.

To make the sauce, heat the butter in a saucepan over medium heat. Add the flour and work into a smooth, creamy paste. Add the rum and stir until smooth. Add the cherries with syrup to the pot. Bring to a gentle boil, reduce heat and cook 2-3 minutes.

Sunday Roasting Hen with Apple Walnut Stuffing

Delicious and elegant! Perfect for holidays, dinner parties or Sunday family dinner!

3 cups country style cubed stuffing
1 cup chopped apples
1 cup celery; thinly sliced
1 cup walnuts; coarsely chopped
¼ cup fresh parsley; chopped
½ teaspoon salt
¼ teaspoon pepper
2 tablespoons butter
1 cup hot water
1 5 - 7 pound roasting hen
1 tablespoon butter; softened
salt and pepper
¼ cup water

Preheat oven to 450°.

Place the cubed stuffing into a large mixing bowl; set aside. Melt the butter in the hot water and add the apple, celery, nuts, parsley, salt and pepper and bring to a slow boil. Cook for 2-3 minutes. Pour hot mixture over cubed stuffing while tossing with a fork. Set aside to cool.

Remove the chicken's innards and discard or save for another use. Wash and pat dry the inside and outside of the hen. Tightly pack the hen's cavity with the stuffing mixture and place into a roasting pan. Rub the top of the hen with the softened margarine and sprinkle lightly with salt and pepper. Pour ¼ cup water in the bottom of the pan.

Place the hen, uncovered into the oven and immediately reduce the heat to 350°. Roast for 20 minutes per pound. Remove from oven and allow to rest for 5 minutes before carving.

Sweet and Sour Chicken

This is a good change for chicken. I like it because the chicken is not breaded, it is just sautéed, and so it does not seem as heavy.

3 ½ tablespoon vegetable oil
2 celery ribs; chopped
1 medium onion; chopped
2 pounds chicken breasts; bone in
1 18-oz. bottle ketchup
1 8-oz. can whole cranberry sauce
1 tablespoon lemon juice
1 teaspoon grated lemon zest
½ teaspoon salt
¼ teaspoon pepper

In a large skillet, or wok, heat 2 tablespoons oil over high heat until hot, swirling to coat sides of pan. Add celery and onion and cook, stirring until soft; 3-4 minutes. Remove to plate.

In the same pan, heat the remaining oil and fry the chicken, turning often, until browned all over; about 6-8 minutes.

In a medium bowl, combine the ketchup, cranberry sauce, lemon juice, lemon zest, salt and pepper. Pour over chicken and cook, covered, over medium-low heat, until chicken is tender, 45-50 minutes, turning occasionally.

Serve with rice.

Chicken, Red Pepper and Zucchini Linguini

This dish is very colorful and looks great on TV! The bonus for you is that it tastes as good as it looks!

4 ounces linguini; cooked according to directions, rinsed under cold water and drained
3 tablespoons olive oil
1 pound chicken breasts; boneless, skinless and cut crosswise into ¼ -inch strips
1 medium zucchini; sliced or cubed
1 medium red pepper; cut into thin strips
1 small onion; chopped
1 clove garlic; minced
1 8-oz. can tomato sauce
1 cup dry white wine
½ teaspoon salt
¼ teaspoon pepper
¼ teaspoon crushed red pepper
½ cup water

Cook pasta as directed above; set aside.

In a large skillet or wok, heat 1 tablespoon of oil over medium-high heat until hot. Add chicken and fry until white, but still juicy; 3-5 minutes. Remove to a plate.

Add the remaining oil over medium-high heat until hot. Add zucchini, red pepper, onion and garlic. Fry until crisp-tender; 3-5 minutes. Add tomato sauce, wine, salt, pepper, red pepper and ½ cup water. Cook 5 minutes.

Return chicken to the pan. Toss in the cooked pasta and cook until heated through; 1-2 minutes. Serve at once.

Chicken with Raspberry Glaze

Beautiful and eloquent but...easy! This one is a winner in my book!

4 skinless, boneless chicken breast halves; pounded ¼-inch thick
½ teaspoon salt
¼ teaspoon pepper
2 tablespoons butter
2 tablespoon vegetable oil
6 green onions (scallions); chopped
1/3 cup raspberry vinegar
½ cup chicken broth
1/3 cup heavy cream
1 tablespoon Dijon mustard
1 cup fresh or frozen raspberries

Wash, pat dry and season the chicken with the salt and pepper. In a large skillet melt 1 tablespoons butter and 1 tablespoon vegetable oil over medium-high heat. Add the chicken, without overlapping, and cook, turning once, until both sides are lightly browned; 6-8 minutes. Remove to a plate.

In the same pan, heat the remaining butter and oil. Sauté the scallions, 1-2 minutes, until soft and fragrant. Stir in the vinegar, chicken broth, cream and mustard. Bring to a boil, reduce heat to medium and boil, 2-3 minutes, until sauce slightly thickens. Return chicken to pan.

Add the raspberries and stir gently. Cook until heated through; 1 minute. To serve, arrange the chicken on a warm platter and pour the sauce over all.

Food Styling Tip

Do not over cook the raspberries! Plus save enough to garnish each serving with three berries and a sprig of parsley!

Curried Apricot Chicken

I first made this dish on HSN using a slow cooker and it was very good. You can also use a slow cooker or prepare it in the oven as directed below. Either way, it's a winner!

1 3 ½ - 4 lb. whole chicken
4 tablespoons apricot all-fruit or preserves
2 teaspoons curry powder
½ teaspoon ground coriander
½ teaspoon ground ginger
¼ teaspoon salt
1 cup chicken broth
1 medium onion; quartered
2 medium cloves garlic
3-4 cups cooked long grain rice
18" length of heavy-duty aluminum foil

Preheat oven to 450°.

In a small glass bowl combine the apricot all-fruit, curry powder, coriander, ginger and salt to make a thin paste; set aside.

Wash chicken thoroughly and pat dry. Place the onion wedges and the whole garlic cloves into the cavity of the chicken. Set chicken into a roasting pan.

Mix 1 tablespoon of the apricot/curry paste into the chicken broth and pour all around the chicken in the pan. Using a basting brush, thoroughly coat chicken with the apricot/curry paste making sure you cover all exposed areas of the chicken.

Tent the chicken with foil, place into the oven and immediately reduce the heat to 350°. Cook 20 minutes per pound, basting occasionally. 30 minutes before the chicken is done; remove foil. Continue cooking, basting often until chicken is browned and tender.

Serve chicken sliced atop hot with fluffy rice; drizzle with the sauce detailed on the next page.

To Make the Sauce:

Separate the fat from the liquid in the pan; discard fat. Remove onions and garlic from the cavity of the chicken and place in a food processor with the separated liquid; process until smooth.

Form a paste by heating 2 tablespoons butter and 2 tablespoons flour in a small saucepan over medium heat. Slowly pour in the processed liquid and bring to a gentle boil for 2-3 three minutes until thick and bubbly.

All American Pot Roast

Stovetop or in a slow cooker, you just can't beat a good pot roast!

3-4 lb. round roast or boneless pot roast
2 Tbsp. vegetable oil
½ cup good red wine
1 clove garlic, minced
1 medium onion, coarsely chopped
1 Tbsp. Worcestershire sauce
1 Tbsp. ketchup
1 Tbsp. *Better Than Bouillon* beef bouillon base
1 tsp. salt
1 tsp. coarse ground black pepper
1 tsp. celery salt
1 cup hot water
½ lb. Baby carrots
10 small red potatoes
1 lb. Whole medium mushrooms
2 stalks celery with leaves, cut into 1" pieces
1 Tbsp. cornstarch or potato starch
¼   cup cold water

Heat oil in a large heavy skillet over medium-low heat. Using long tongs, carefully brown roast about 1 minute on each side and end. Remove roast and set inside your 7 Qt. Slow cooker or large Dutch oven.

Add wine to the skillet and scrape bottom with spatula. Add onion and garlic, simmer 1 minute. Add next the next 7 ingredients; stir. Pour mixture over roast.   Cover and cook in the slow cooker on low for 4-5 hours or on the stove top for 1 ½ -2 hours. Arrange the vegetables around the roast and slow cook another 2 ½ hours or 1 hour on the stovetop.

Remove roast and vegetables to a large platter; cover with foil to keep warm.

For Gravy: If using a slow cooker, transfer the liquid to a saucepan for stovetop, leave the liquid in the pot; heat liquid to boiling. In a small bowl or cup mix cornstarch and water together, pour into bubbling liquid; stir until gravy thickens; pour over roast and vegetables.

● ●

Spanish Beef

I love this Spanish version of a beef stew. It has great a great flavor and make wonderful leftovers. Try this one in a slow cooker as I do on HSN!

3 pounds round steak; cut into serving sized pieces
½ cup flour
2 tablespoons olive oil
2 tablespoon butter
1 large Spanish onion; cut into thin rings.
2 cloves garlic
¼ cup dry red cooking wine
2 14.5-oz. cans diced tomatoes
¼ cup beef broth
1 bay leaf
½ teaspoon thyme
2 tablespoons capers
¼ cup stuffed green olives, coarsely chopped

Place flour and meat pieces in large plastic bag and shake until meat is coated. Heat olive oil and butter in large heavy skillet over medium heat. Lightly brown the meat in small batches and place into a large Dutch oven or Slow Cooker.

When all the meat is browned, add the onion and garlic to the pan and cook for about 3 minutes. Add the wine quickly; scraping the bottom of the skillet. Add the tomatoes, beef broth, thyme and bay leaf; bring mixture to a boil.   Pour tomato mixture over meat.

On the stovetop, bring the mixture to a boil, cover and reduce heat to medium low. Cook for 2 hours adding the capers and olives during the final 30 minutes of cooking. Or, if using a slow cooker, cook on Low for 6–7 hours adding the capers and olives during the final hour of cooking.

Serve with rice.

Cheesy Shepard's Pie

A couple of years ago, I went to London several times to work on another shopping channel. While there, I fell in love with the Shepard's Pie. Although my version is a bit Americanized, it really hits the spot on a cold, rainy day and makes me think of Pub fare!

2 pounds. lean ground beef
2 tablespoons butter
1 medium onion; finely chopped
1 1-pound bag frozen peas and carrots
1 10.5-oz. can double strength beef broth
1 tablespoon flour
1 tablespoon Worcestershire sauce
1 teaspoon salt
½ teaspoon coarse ground black pepper
2 tablespoons ketchup
4 cups mashed potatoes; instant or homemade
2 cups sharp cheddar cheese; shredded

Preheat oven to 375°.

In a large heavy skillet, over medium heat, brown beef. Drain and set aside. Wipe out the pan and melt 2 tablespoons butter over medium heat. Stir in the onions and sauté gently for 2-3 minutes. Cook the frozen peas and carrots in lightly salted boiling water for 2 minutes, drain and add to the onions. Cook for another 1-2 minutes.

In a measuring cup or small bowl, whisk together the canned beef broth with the flour until blended. Pour over the vegetables. Stir in the Worcestershire sauce and the ketchup. Bring to a gentle boil, cover, reduce heat and cook for 20 minutes. Add the beef and mix well. Spread the beef and vegetable mixture into the bottom a slightly greased 9x11-inch oven-safe glass baking dish.

Spread the hot mashed potatoes over all. Top with cheese. Place into the preheated oven and bake 20-30 minutes or until potatoes and cheese are lightly browned and the edges look bubbly.

Sunday Beef Roast with Vegetables

A great dinner and then terrific sandwiches the day after!

3-4 lb. sirloin tip or eye of round roast
1 tablespoon olive oil
1 tablespoon dried rosemary
1 teaspoon coarse salt; sea or kosher
½ teaspoon coarse ground black pepper
1 tablespoon vegetable oil
1 tablespoon balsamic vinegar
¼ cup good red wine
¼ cup water
1 clove garlic
1 tablespoon Worcestershire sauce
1 teaspoon salt
1 teaspoon coarse ground black pepper
4 carrots; peeled and cut into three pieces
6 medium red potatoes; quartered
2 medium onions; peeled and quartered
2 tablespoons flour
1 ½ cup hot water

Remove roast from refrigerator, place on a rack inside a large shallow roasting pan and allow to sit at room temperature, uncovered, for 2 hours. Rub the meat with the oil and then sprinkle and press in the salt, pepper and rosemary.

Preheat oven to 500°. Place the roast into the oven and immediately reduce the heat to 350°. The meat will need to roast for 20 minutes per pound for a medium rare center.

In a blender or food processor, blend until smooth the oil, vinegar, wine, water, garlic, Worcestershire sauce, salt and pepper. Set a side.

45 minutes before the roast is done, remove it from the oven and arrange the vegetables around the rack. Pour the liquid mixture over the vegetables, return to oven and continue cooking until desired doneness is achieved; a meat thermometer should read between 140° for rare up to 170° for well done. Transfer meat and vegetables to a large platter.

● ●

To make to a savory gravy, pour off all but 2 tablespoons of the liquid. Place the roaster pan on the stovetop over medium-high heat (or transfer liquid and bottom scrapings to a saucepan if you must). Stir in 2 tablespoons flour. Pour in the hot water, and bring to a boil, constantly scraping the bottom of the pan. Cook about 5 minutes until mixture begins to thicken. Add a little Kitchen Bouquet if a darker color is desired. Pour gravy through a sieve into a gravy boat, mashing the sieve with a spoon to get all the liquid.

Slice the roast thinly and with the gravy on the side. Pass around horseradish if desired.

Steak Diane

I've often wondered whom Diane is that she has such a tasty dish named for her! Do you know?

4 tablespoons butter
4 tablespoons chopped green onions
4 6-8-oz. beef filets or tenderloins
8 tablespoons butter
3 tablespoons Worcestershire sauce
3 dashes Tabasco
1 cup fresh parsley; chopped
salt and pepper

In a large skillet, melt 4 tablespoons of butter, over medium heat, and sauté the onions until tender but not brown. Remove onions from the pan and set aside.

Slicing against the grain, cut the filets into 3 or 4 slices. Add 8 tablespoons butter to the pan over medium heat. Add the meat and brown for about 3 minutes on each side; remove from pan.

Add the Worcestershire sauce, Tabasco and parsley to the butter in the pan. Stir and then put the steak and onions back in. Cook for another 6 minutes, turning steaks once. Salt and pepper to taste.

Serve with hot buttered noodles and a green vegetable.

• •

Oriental Pepper Beef with Noodles

On HSN, I make the beef mixture in my slow cooker and then toss in the noodles at the last minute! It looks great and tastes even better!

2 pounds beef flank steak
1 tablespoons vegetable oil
1 tablespoon butter
1 10.5-ounce can double strength beef broth
¼ cup low-sodium soy sauce
¼ cup no-pulp orange juice
½ cup water
1 teaspoon ground ginger
2 cloves garlic; chopped
1 tablespoon butter
1 large onion; coarsely chopped
1 medium red pepper; coarsely chopped
1 medium green pepper; coarsely chopped
1lb. linguini noodles; cooked al dente and drained.

Cut flank steak, across the grain, into thin, 2-inch slices.

Heat the butter and oil, over medium-high heat, in a large deep skillet. Add the beef and cook, stirring constantly, for 3-4 minutes or until lightly browned. Add in the broth, soy sauce, orange juice, water, ginger and garlic. Heat to a boil, cover, reduce heat to medium-low and simmer 30 minutes.

Heat in a small skillet, over medium, 1 tablespoon butter. Add the onions and peppers and sauté for just 2-3 minutes or until the peppers colors brighten and the onion is softened. Add into the beef and broth. Cover and simmer another 15 minutes.

Toss in the cooked pasta and cook just until heated through and the pasta begins to absorb a little of the liquid. Serve immediately.

Beef Stroganoff

My Mom always made me this on my birthday because I liked it so much!   Now, when I make it for myself, I always make enough for leftovers!

4 tablespoons extra virgin olive oil
4 tablespoons butter
1 ½ pounds lean sirloin steak; thinly sliced across the grain
¼ cup onion, finely chopped
¾ pound fresh mushrooms; thinly sliced
1 clove garlic; finely minced
½ teaspoon salt
2 tablespoons Worcestershire sauce
¼ teaspoon black pepper
¼ cup dry white wine
¼ cup water
1 cup sour cream
½ pound wide egg noodles; cooked and drained

Melt half of the butter and half of the olive oil in large non-stick skillet over medium heat. Add beef and sauté until done; about 6 minutes. Drain beef; wipe pan clean.

Add the remaining oil and butter and heat over medium. Add onion, mushrooms and garlic and sauté for 1-2 minutes or until the mushrooms soften. Add drained beef, Worcestershire sauce, salt and pepper. Stir and cook for another minute. Add wine and water, cover and reduce heat to med-low. Simmer uncovered for 15 minutes.

Add sour cream to beef and cook until just warmed through. Serve over warm buttered wide egg noodles.

Rotisserie Roast Beef

If you own a rotisserie, like the one I present on HSN, you will love this recipe. It makes the perfect roasts and a beautiful presentation for a dinner party.

3 lb. Sirloin tip or eye of round roast
1 Tbsp. olive oil
1 Tbsp. rosemary leaves
2 tsp. thyme
½ tsp. rubbed sage
1 tsp. oregano
2 tsp. garlic salt
1 tsp. coarsely ground black pepper

Skewer the beef onto the rotisserie prongs; lock end into place. Rub the entire surface of the beef with the olive oil. Mix the remaining seasoning together and sprinkle evenly over roast pressing the seasonings lightly into the roast for better sticking.

Insert rotisserie attachment into the oven. Turn the oven to 450, rotisserie and stay on settings. Turn the convection feature on. Cook for 30 minutes then reduce heat to 375, turn off convection feature and continue cooking until desired internal temperature is achieved; about 40 minutes more for medium-rare.

Carefully remove rotisserie from oven and set onto a large cutting board. Disengage the end and slide, using a fork, the beef off the prongs and onto the board. Wait 5-10 minutes before cutting.

Serve with Creamy Horseradish Sauce:

½ cup sour cream
2 tbsp. prepared horseradish
1 tbsp. dried parsley flakes
1 tsp. Worcestershire sauce

Home-Style Meatloaf

Using this recipe, I have sold thousands and thousands of my
Bravetti hand mixer on HSN for one simple reason...no one wants
to put their hands into the raw egg and meat!
Using the dough hooks that come with my mixer, you don't have to!

3 lbs. lean ground beef
1 medium onion; finely chopped
1 medium green bell pepper; finely chopped
1 clove garlic; minced
¼ cup ketchup, plus extra for the top
2 large eggs
2 tablespoon Worcestershire sauce
1 teaspoon Salt
¼ teaspoon black pepper
3 slices white bread; torn into small pieces
1 tablespoon milk

Preheat oven to 375°.

Moisten the bread pieces in the milk.

In a large mixing bowl, divide and layer the meat with the
moistened breadcrumbs so you have about 3 layers. Add the onion,
peppers, garlic, ketchup, eggs, Worcestershire sauce, salt and
pepper. Use the dough hooks of your mixer and blend the
ingredients together on the lowest speed. If you don't have my
Bravetti mixer, you'll have to use your hands! Just be gentle with
the mixture so you don't toughen the meat.

Form the meat into a loaf and place it in a lightly greased 9x9-inch
or 7 ½ x 10-inch baking dish. Spread a little ketchup on the top and
bake for 1 hour or until a meat thermometer reads 160° when
inserted into the middle. Do not overcook; you do not want a dry
meatloaf!

Hint: After about 45 minutes, remove the meatloaf from the oven,
carefully pour off the excess fat and take a temperature reading.
This way, you won't overcook it and it has a chance to brown more
on the bottom with the fat removed!

Serve with mashed potatoes and green beans!

Italian Meatballs

You can make these any size you want! Use them as appetizers, with pasta or make my favorite...meatball hoagies!

3 lbs. lean ground beef
1 medium onion; very finely chopped
3 cloves garlic; minced
1 small can tomato paste; about 1/3 cup
2 large eggs
3 tablespoons Italian seasoning
1 teaspoon oregano
1 teaspoon basil
1 teaspoon Salt
¼ teaspoon black pepper
¼ teaspoon crushed red pepper
3 slices white bread; torn into small pieces
1 tablespoon milk
2 tablespoons olive oil for frying

Moisten the bread pieces in the milk.

In a large mixing bowl, divide and layer the meat with the moistened breadcrumbs so you have about 3 layers. Add the onion, garlic, tomato paste, eggs and all seasonings.

Use the dough hooks of your mixer and blend the ingredients together on the lowest speed. If you don't have my Bravetti mixer, you'll have to use your hands! Just be gentle with the mixture so you don't toughen the meat.

Form the meatballs to the size you want. Heat the olive oil over medium high heat in a large skillet. Working in batches, quickly fry the meatballs, turning often so they don't get a flat side, until they are browned all over. Drain on paper towels.

Note: If you are making these to go into a sauce, lower them into the sauce and simmer 20-30 minutes. However, if you are making these to eat plain or serve with sauce on the side, place the meatballs on a broiler pan and bake at 350° until they are done...the time will vary according to size!

• •

Oven Baked Barbeque Brisket

You have to start this the night before, but it makes the best barbeque sandwich I've ever had! I've often had guests ask me which smokehouse I bought it from!

4-6 pound beef brisket; trimmed
½ teaspoon garlic salt
½ teaspoon onion salt
½ teaspoon celery salt
1 4-oz. bottle Liquid Smoke; save 3 teaspoons for the sauce

Sauce

2 cups ketchup
½ cup vinegar
½ cup sugar
¼ teaspoon garlic salt
¼ teaspoon onion salt
¼ teaspoon celery salt
3 teaspoons Liquid Smoke
½ cup Worcestershire sauce

In a large oven-safe Dutch oven or roasting pan, place the brisket. Sprinkle with the seasonings and coat all over with the Liquid Smoke. Cover with foil and refrigerate overnight.

The next day, preheat oven to 250°.

Remove the brisket from the refrigerator and pour off and remaining marinade.

Prepare the sauce by heating all the ingredients together in a saucepan until the sugar is dissolved. Generously coat the entire brisket with sauce; you'll only use about half. Cover with foil and bake in the preheated oven for 5 to 6 hours.

Slice and serve with the remaining sauce.

Serving Suggestion: In Texas they serve this either with slices of white bread, or on buns, with dill pickle slices and thinly sliced onion!

● ●

Country Fried Steak

In some parts of the country this is called chicken-fried steak! Whatever you call it, it's my daughter Merritt's favorite meal when served with mashed potatoes, cream gravy and buttered corn. Whenever she comes home from college, I always try to make it for her!

6 thin cubed steaks; about 1 ½ pounds
salt and pepper
flour for dusting
1 egg
1 cup milk
2 cups all-purpose flour
1 teaspoon seasoning salt (I use Lawry's)
½ teaspoon black pepper
¼ -½ cup vegetable oil

Wash, pat dry and very lightly salt and pepper both sides of the steak. Dust with flour and sit on a wire rack to dry.

Beat together the egg and milk; set aside.

Stir together, on a plate, the remaining flour, seasoning salt and pepper.

Heat over medium-high, in a large heavy skillet, just enough oil to cover the bottom of the pan. When the oil shimmers, dip the steaks, one at a time, into the milk mixture, dredge in the seasoned flour and place in the pan; lower the heat to medium. You don't want to crowd the pan so you may have to fry in batches adding oil if necessary.

Fry 4 minutes on one side, turn, and fry another 3-4 minutes until the steak is a deep golden brown and no juices rise to the top.

Drain on paper towels using an extra towel to blot any oil from the top of the steak.

Serve with country-style cream gravy; see index for recipe.

Southern Style Liver 'n Onions

Not everyone likes Liver 'n Onions the way my Mother and I do, but if you do, then you'll love this family recipe...straight from the old South!

1 pound calves liver; about 4 thin slices
salt and pepper
flour for dusting
1 very large yellow onion; cut into ½ -inch thick rings
4 slices of bacon
½ cup hot water

Wash, pat dry and lightly salt and pepper the liver. Lightly dust with flour.

In a large, heavy skillet, fry the bacon over medium heat until crispy. Remove and drain on a paper towel. Increase the heat a little. You want the grease hot but not to the point of burning.

Add the prepared liver to the pan and sear, turning once, about 2-3 minutes per side or until edges are browned. Remove and drain on paper towel.

Add the onion to the pan and cook 3-4 minutes until the onion is softened and beginning to turn translucent in the center and brown on the edges.

Add the hot water and scrape the bottom. Place the liver and bacon back into the pan, reduce the heat and cook about 5-6 minutes or until liver is done. Do not overcook or the meat will be very tough.

Serve the liver and onions very hot. It's up to you if you want to eat the bacon, some people do and some people don't!

NY Strips in Mushroom Wine Sauce

This is a very simple way to have a great tasting steak...without grilling. Use a stainless steel pan for this so you can deglaze and prepare the savory sauce!

2 tablespoons butter
1 pound fresh mushrooms; sliced thin
1 clove garlic; minced
2 NY strip steaks; medium-thick
salt and pepper
1 tablespoon olive oil
½ cup good red wine
½ cup hot water
1 tablespoon Better than Bouillon Beef Base
2 teaspoons Worcestershire sauce
1 tablespoon balsamic vinegar
½ teaspoon salt
¼ teaspoon pepper
2 teaspoons cornstarch
1 tablespoon water

30 minutes before cooking, remove steaks from the refrigerator, wash, pat dry, lightly salt and pepper and allow to sit on a plate, at room temperature for a half hour.

In a large stainless steel skillet, melt the butter over medium heat. Add the mushrooms and garlic and sauté 3-4 minutes or until the mushrooms are soft but not brown. Remove the mushrooms from the pan and set aside. Add the olive oil to the pan and increase the heat to medium-high. When the oil is hot, add the steaks and cook for 3 minutes. Turn and cook 3 more minutes. Remove from pan and set aside.

Quickly add the wine to the pan and scrape the bottom. Add the water, bouillon, Worcestershire sauce, vinegar, salt and pepper. Bring to a boil, reduce heat to medium and simmer about 10 minutes to reduce the liquid; the liquid should be very bubbly. Add the steaks and mushrooms and continue to cook another 5-6 minutes or until the steaks are done to your liking. Transfer the steaks to warmed plates and pour the sauce over all.

● ●

Veal Piccata

This lemony dish is so good it makes my mouth water just writing about it!

1 ½ pounds veal cutlets
1 teaspoon salt
¼ teaspoon pepper
¼ cup flour
2 tablespoons butter
2 tablespoons olive oil
½ cup dry white wine
1 cup chicken stock or broth
3 tablespoons fresh lemon juice
2 tablespoons capers; rinsed and drained
1 tablespoon fresh parsley; finely chopped

Pound the veal between two pieces of waxed paper ¼ - inch thickness. Cut each cutlet in half. Season the pieces with ¾ teaspoon salt and ¼ teaspoon pepper and dust lightly with flour; shake off excess.

In a large non-reactive skillet, melt 1 tablespoon butter with 1 tablespoon olive oil over medium heat. Add as many veal pieces as will fit without overcrowding and cook 2 minutes on each side, or until lightly browned. Remove veal to a warmed platter and cover with foil to keep warm. Repeat until all the veal is cooked, adding oil and butter as needed.

Add the wine to the pan and bring to a boil, scraping up the bits stuck to the bottom of the pan. Add stock and boil 4 to 5 minutes to reduce the liquid to ¾ cup.

Add the lemon juice and capers to the pan and cook 1 minute. Return veal to pan and heat through. Season with the remaining ¼ teaspoon salt and garnish with fresh parsley. Serve immediately.

Veal Marsala

I was always so excited when my Mom would make this for us...I just love it!

1 ½ pounds veal cutlets
½ teaspoon salt
¼ teaspoon pepper
¼ cup flour
2 tablespoons butter
2 tablespoons olive oil
½ cup dry Marsala wine or dry sherry
1 cup chicken stock or broth

Season the pieces with salt and pepper and dust lightly with flour; shake off excess.

In a large non-reactive skillet, melt 1 tablespoon butter with 1 tablespoon olive oil over medium heat. Add as many veal pieces as will fit without overcrowding and cook 4 minutes or until lightly browned on both sides. Remove veal to a warmed platter and cover with foil to keep warm. Repeat until all the veal is cooked, adding oil and butter as needed.

Add the wine to the pan and bring to a boil, scraping up the bits stuck to the bottom of the pan. Add stock and boil 3 to 4 minutes to reduce the liquid to ½ cup.

Return veal to pan and heat throughout. Season with additional salt and pepper as needed.

Variation: Sauté ½ pound fresh sliced mushrooms in the butter and oil after the veal has been removed and continue as directed.

Veal Chops Stuffed with Prosciutto and Gorgonzola

This is a meal fit for a king...or queen!

2 veal loin chops, cut ¾ -inch thick; about 12 ounces each
1 thin slice of prosciutto or ham; cut in half
2 tablespoons crumbled gorgonzola or blue cheese
2 tablespoons olive oil
1 ½ teaspoons chopped fresh rosemary (or ½ teaspoon dried)
1/8 teaspoon pepper
½ cup dry white wine

Trim the excess fat from the veal. With a small knife, slit a pocket in the meaty part of each chop; cut towards the bone. Stuff pockets with prosciutto and cheese; fasten closed with toothpicks.

In a large skillet, heat olive oil. Cook chops over medium-high heat turning once, about 4 minutes or until the outside is browned.

Sprinkle rosemary and pepper onto the veal and pour the wine into the pan. Bring to a boil, cover, reduce heat and cook, turning once, 10-15 minutes or until veal is cooked through but still juicy.

Serve immediately with oven roasted potatoes.

Lamb Chops with Mint Pesto

This dish is so good, there won't be any leftovers!

1 cup packed fresh mint leaves
½ cup fresh parsley leaves
¼ cup walnuts
3 cloves garlic
1 cup plus 2 tablespoons extra-virgin olive oil
2 tablespoons white wine vinegar
1 ¾ teaspoons salt
½ teaspoon pepper
8 lamb shoulder chops; about 7 ounces each

Mint Pesto

Place the mint, parsley, walnuts and garlic into a food processor and chop. With the machine on, slowly pour in 1 cup of the olive oil and continue to process until mixture is very finely chopped but not pureed. Season with the vinegar, ¾ teaspoon salt and ¼ teaspoon pepper. Set the mint pesto aside.

Lamb Chops

Light a hot fire on your grill, or preheat your broiler. Trim the excess fat from the chops and rub with the remaining olive oil. Season with the remaining salt and pepper.

Grill or broil the chops 3 inches from the heat 4 minutes. Turn and cook another 2 minutes for medium rare, or until cooked to desired doneness. Serve with mint pesto.

Serving Suggestion: This is great with garlic mashed potatoes!

Food Styling Tip

To serve, place a mound of mashed potatoes in the middle of the plate. Place 2 chops, slightly overlapping, atop the potatoes. Drizzle pesto around the outer edge of the plate and on top of the chops. Garnish with a sprig of mint.

Rack of Lamb

I used to think I made a good rack of lamb. Then I visited London a few times and learned their secret for the best tasting lamb I've ever had! Try it for yourself!

1 young rack of lamb; about 6 chops
2 cloves garlic
¼ cup melted butter
½ teaspoon salt
½ teaspoon coarse ground black pepper
1 ½ teaspoons dried rosemary leaves

Preheat oven to 400°.

Wash and pat dry the rack of lamb. Place, bone side down, on a metal rack in a shallow roasting pan.

Peel the garlic and cut each clove in half lengthwise and then half again lengthwise.
Using a small sharp knife, make 8 small slits evenly across the meat and insert a piece of garlic into each slit.

Brush the meat with the melted butter and season with the salt, pepper and rosemary.

Place the lamb into the oven and roast about 25 minutes or until the internal temperature reaches 145° on a meat thermometer.

Carve into chops and serve.

Serving suggestion: Make a mint pesto sauce (see recipe index). Lightly spread some on the plate where the chops will sit and drizzle a little on top of the chops.

Barbeque Pork Pull-Apart

This tastes great and cooks pretty quickly in a pressure cooker!

3 ½ lb. pork shoulder blade roast
1 medium onion
1 can or bottle beer (16 oz.)
1 cup water
1 Tbsp. liquid smoke
1 tsp. Kosher salt
1 tsp. coarse ground pepper
1 bottle (18 oz.) barbeque sauce (your favorite brand of bottled sauce)

Thoroughly wash and pat dry the roast.

Pour beer, water, liquid smoke, salt and pepper into a large Dutch oven or pressure cooker. Turn heat to medium-low, stir and allow bubbles to subside.

Add the pork roast and the onion, increase heat and bring to a boil. Cover, reduce heat and simmer 2 ½ hours in a Dutch oven or 1 hour 15 minutes in a pressure cooker.

Remove roast from pan and place onto a cutting board. Discard liquid in pan. Remove bone and any large fat portions from roast. Using two large forks, shred meat; or chop if you prefer.

You may serve the meat as is, drizzle barbeque sauce on each serving, or return meat to pan and add barbeque sauce, mixing well. Cover and cook on low. Serve on buns. Serve with additional sauce, dill pickle slices and thinly sliced onion, if desired.

Variation: Instead of using bottled barbeque sauce, make your own Homemade Barbeque Sauce!

Pork Cutlets with Lemon Caper Sauce

This dish is very good, easy to make and much less expensive than the similar Veal Piccata!

8 thin slices boneless pork loin; 1 ½ - 2 pounds
½ teaspoon salt
½ teaspoon pepper
¼ cup flour
2 eggs beaten with 1 tablespoon water
1 ½ cups dry bread crumbs; spread out on a plate or piece of waxed paper
2 – 4 tablespoons olive oil
6 tablespoons butter
2 lemons; 1 juiced and 1 sliced
3 tablespoons capers; rinsed and drained

Preheat oven to 350°.

Wash, pat dry and season meat with salt and pepper. Dust with flour, dip into the egg-water mixture and then dredge in the breadcrumbs to coat; pat gently to help the breadcrumbs adhere.

In a large skillet, heat 2 tablespoons olive oil over medium-high heat. Add as many pieces as will fit without overcrowding the pan and cook 1 ½ minutes on each side; transfer to a baking sheet. Continue to cook the rest of the pork, adding oil as needed. Place pan into the oven and bake 10 minutes.

Wipe out the skillet and heat 6 tablespoons butter over medium heat until it begins to brown. Immediately add the lemon juice and the capers.

Arrange the pork on a platter and pour the sauce over all. Garnish with lemon slices.

Italian-Spiced Pork Chops

I love pork chops on the grill but when I don't want to go to the trouble of cooking outside, I make them this way! They are juicy and tender and have a very good flavor.

1 pound boneless loin chops; about ½-inch thick
½ teaspoon salt
1 tablespoon Italian seasoning
2 tablespoons olive oil
1 medium onion; chopped
1 14.5-oz can Italian style stewed tomatoes
¼ cup water

Wash and pat dry the chops. Season both sides with salt and Italian seasoning.
Heat olive oil in a large non-stick skillet over medium-high heat. When oil is hot add chops and sear for 1-2 minutes on each side and remove to plate.

Reduce heat to medium, add a little more oil if needed and sauté onion and garlic for 2-3 minutes or until onion is soft. Add in the tomatoes and water. Replace the chops spooning liquid over the top.

Bring mixture to a boil, cover and reduce heat to medium-low. Simmer 30 minutes or until chops are done. Add salt and pepper to taste.

Serve with hot fluffy white rice.

Tangy Pork Loin Roast

This tastes almost like a barbeque you sauce...only very tangy!

4 pounds boneless pork loin
1 teaspoon garlic salt
1 teaspoons chili powder
1 cup apple jelly
1 cup ketchup
2 tablespoons cider vinegar
3 teaspoons chili powder

Preheat oven to 400°.

Wash and pat dry the roast. Rub the surface of the roast with the garlic salt and 1 teaspoon chili powder. Place the pork in a roasting pan and put into the oven. Immediately reduce the heat to 325° and cook for 1 hour.

Combine the apple jelly, ketchup, vinegar and chili powder in a saucepan. Simmer over low heat for 15 minutes, stirring occasionally. Pour half the sauce over the roast and continue cooking until roast is done; 35-40 minutes per pound total cooking time.

Remove pork to serving platter. Bring the remaining sauce to a boil and serve with the roast.

Baby Back Ribs – Asian & Traditional

These are so yummy! You can cook them on the grill for the last fifteen minutes (watch them carefully!), or do as I do and cook them right in the oven!

4-5 pounds baby back pork ribs

Asian Style

1 ½ cups ketchup
1 ½ cups soy sauce
½ cup honey
1/3 cup dry sherry
3 tablespoons gingerroot; minced
1 tablespoon minced garlic

Arrange the ribs in a large shallow dish. Combine the remaining ingredients in a bowl and mix well. Pour over the ribs, turning to coat. Marinade the ribs in the refrigerator, loosely covered, for 8 – 10 hours, turning occasionally.

Wipe the excess marinade from the ribs and place them in a large shallow roasting pan.

Cover with foil and bake at 325° for 1 hour. Uncover, baste liberally with the sauce, increase heat to 400° and bake an additional 15 minutes or until they start to crisp around the edges; basting every 5 minutes.

If you want to cook these on the grill, baste and place them on a moderately hot grill after the first hour of oven cooking. Grill, basting and turning twice, 10-15 minutes or until crispy around the edges.

Traditional

For traditional Barbeque ribs, use the Barbeque Sauce recipe in the index and follow the directions above.

Pork Roast with Honey Mustard Glaze

This is my favorite pork roast! The mustard gives it a delicious flavor as well as an appealing color.

1 pork loin or shoulder
3 tablespoons Dijon Mustard
2 tablespoon honey
1 clove garlic; minced
2 teaspoons dried rosemary leaves
½ teaspoon salt
¼ cup flour

Remove pork from refrigerator 1 hour before cooking, wash and pat dry.

Preheat oven to 450°.

Make a paste with the mustard, honey, garlic, rosemary and salt. Using your hands, rub the pork all over with the mixture. Use a sifter and lightly cover the roast with the flour.

Place the roast, fat side up on a rack in a greased shallow roasting pan. Place into oven and immediately reduce heat to 325°. Cook, uncovered 25 to 35 minutes per pound depending on size and cut of the meat. The internal temperature should be 170° for a loin roast and 185° for a shoulder roast.

Remove from oven and let rest for 10 minutes before carving.

To make a gravy, see the Pan Gravy for Beef recipe in the index.

Southern-Fried Pork Chops

Fried Pork Chops, served with rice and tomato gravy is my Father's favorite meal so needless to say and my Mom made it often! Lucky for me that I also adore it!

1 pound thin cut pork chops; bone in
1 cup all-purpose flour
1 teaspoon salt
½ teaspoon black pepper
vegetable oil for frying

Wash and pat dry the pork chops. Mix the flour with the salt and pepper and spread on a plate. Dredge the pork chops in the seasoned flour to completely coat; shake off excess.

Heat enough oil to just cover the bottom of a large skillet over medium-high heat. Place the chops in the pan, without overcrowding, reduce heat to medium and fry 3-4 minutes on each side or until done and golden brown. Remove from pan and drain on paper towels.

Make pan gravy or serve Southern-style with tomato gravy!

Ham and Scalloped Potatoes

This makes a great meal the whole family will love; even the little ones! Plus, it makes great use of your leftover holiday ham!

3 cups thin potato slices
1 teaspoon salt
2 tablespoons flour
3-6 tablespoons butter
¼ cup green onion; sliced
1 cup ham; diced
1 ¼ cups milk or cream
¼ cup shredded Swiss cheese
½ teaspoon salt
¼ teaspoon paprika
¼ teaspoon dry mustard

Preheat oven to 350°.

Drop the sliced potatoes into boiling water with 1 teaspoon salt added. Cook for 8 minutes and drain well. In a greased 10-inch baking dish, place the potatoes in three layers adding to each layer a sprinkling of flour, dots of butter, onion and ham.

Heat the milk or cream with the cheese, salt, paprika and mustard until the cheese has melted. Pour evenly over the potatoes.

Bake about 35-40 minutes or until fork tender and browned around the edges.

Baked Holiday Ham

You can decorate the top of this ham with pineapple rings, cranberries or orange slices for a very festive holiday ham!

4 pound whole or shank ham labeled "fully cooked"
1 1/3 cup brown sugar
2 teaspoons dry mustard
3 tablespoons ham drippings
whole cloves

Preheat oven to 325°.

Place the ham on a rack, uncovered, in a shallow pan. Bake.

For a whole ham, allow 15-18 minutes per pound and for a shank (half ham) allow 18-24 minute per pound. Either way the internal temperature should reach 140°.

30 minutes before ham is finished cooking, remove from oven.

Increase heat to 425°.

Remove rind from the ham, all but a collar around the shank bone. With a sharp knife, make diagonal slashes across the fat topside of the ham to make diamond shapes.

Make a glaze with the brown sugar, mustard and pan drippings. Rub the glaze all over the top of the ham. Insert whole cloves at fat diamond intersections and decorate with fruit slices as desired.

Reduce heat again to 325° and return the ham to the oven for 30 minutes. Place on platter and garnish as desired or see the photo in the photo inserts for garnish ideas.

Fettuccine with Alfredo or Romano Sauce

This true, basic version of fettuccine Alfredo just tosses the pasta with the cheese. I prefer a cream version that comes from Rome. Both recipes are listed below, so choose your favorite style...both are very rich and delicious

1 pound fresh fettuccine

Boil the fettuccine in a large pot of salted water until tender but still firm; about 4 minutes. Drain.

Alfredo Sauce:

2 sticks butter
2 cups grated Parmesan cheese

Melt butter in a large skillet over medium; do not allow it to brown. Remove from heat and add cooked pasta to the butter. Sprinkle on the cheese and toss until all pasta is well coated with the butter and cheese.

Romano Sauce:

6 tablespoons butter
2 cups heavy cream
¾ cup grated Parmesan cheese
black pepper

Melt butter in a large skillet over medium. Add cream and bring to a boil . Cook until reduced to about 1 ½ cups, 4 to 5 minutes; be careful not to let it boil over. Stir in half the cheese and cook 1 to 2 minutes. Add cooked pasta to pan and toss well. Pass the remaining cheese with a pepper mill on the side.

Spaghetti with Puttanesca Sauce

This quick and spicy dish is one of my very favorites!

2 tablespoons olive oil
3 cloves garlic; peeled and thinly sliced
¼ teaspoon red pepper flakes
6 flat anchovy filets; finely chopped (if you omit these add ¼ teaspoon salt)
1 6 ½ - oz. jar oil-cured black olives; pitted
1 tablespoon capers
1 28-oz. can Italian peeled tomatoes; drained and chopped
¼ teaspoon salt
¼ teaspoon pepper
1 pound spaghetti; cooked al dente and drained

In large skillet, heat olive oil over medium heat. Stir in garlic, hot pepper flakes and anchovies. Cook about 1 minute. Add olives, capers and tomatoes. Cook, stirring occasionally, 8 to 10 minutes or until sauce thickens. Season with salt and pepper to taste.

Meanwhile cook the pasta in salted boiling water until tender but firm; drain.

Pour the pasta and sauce into a large warmed bowl and toss together. Serve hot with freshly grated Parmesan cheese.

Fusilli with Carbonara Sauce

This creamy dish is absolutely wonderful. You can serve it with any pasta like penne, fettuccini or bowtie if you prefer, but try to use prosciutto instead of ham if possible.

4 tablespoons butter
1 clove garlic; minced
1 ½ cups heavy cream
1 cup frozen peas
6 ounces sliced prosciutto or other ham; cut into slices
½ cup grated Parmesan cheese
1 pound fusilli pasta

Melt butter with the garlic in a large skillet over medium. Add cream and bring to a boil. Cook 3 minutes to thicken; be careful not to let it boil over. Add peas and prosciutto and cook 1 to 2 minutes. Remove from heat and add 2 tablespoons of the cheese.

Meanwhile cook pasta in rapidly boiling, salted, water until tender but still firm; about 10-12 minutes. Drain.

Add cooked pasta to the sauce and toss well. Pass the remaining cheese on the side.

Marinara Sauce

This versatile tomato-based sauce is great alone with pasta or can be used as a base for many other pasta sauces or in baked pasta dishes. This makes 5 to 6 cups so adjust the recipe for the quantity needed.

1 tablespoon butter
2 tablespoons olive oil
2 cloves garlic; chopped
3 flat anchovy filets; chopped
2 tablespoons tomato paste
2 30-oz. cans Italian crushed tomatoes in puree
1 cup water
2 tablespoons fresh parsley
2 teaspoons dried oregano
1 teaspoon dried basil
½ teaspoon salt
¼ teaspoon pepper

In a large non-reactive sauce pan, melt the butter with the olive oil over medium heat. Stir in garlic and cook 1 minute, being careful not to burn. Stir in anchovy until dissolved, 1 to 2 minutes.

Add tomato paste and stir to heat. Stir in tomatoes with puree, water, parsley, oregano, basil, salt and pepper. Bring to a boil and simmer uncovered 30 minutes.

Italian Meat Sauce

This hearty sauce can be used over spaghetti, as a base to homemade lasagna or to bake with Rigatoni, Ziti and Penne.

1 tablespoon olive oil
1 large onion; chopped
½ green pepper; chopped
1 pound mild Italian Sausage; casings removed
1 pound lean ground beef
6 cups Marinara Sauce (see recipe index)
1 cup water
2 teaspoons dried basil
1 teaspoon dried oregano

In a large non-reactive sauce pan, heat oil over medium heat. Sauté onion and pepper for 2-3 minutes or until soft. Remove from pan, set aside.

Brown the sausage over medium heat 6-8 minutes, drain and set aside. Brown the ground beef 5-6 minutes, drain and return to pan. Add the sausage, onions and pepper back to the pan and stir to mix.

Pour in the Marinara Sauce and water. Add the basil and oregano. Bring mixture to a boil, reduce heat, partially cover and cook on a low simmer for 30 minutes. Uncover, increase heat to medium and cook, stirring occasionally, until sauce thickens, about 6 to 8 minutes.

Lazy-Day Lasagna

Using a jarred sauce and the no-cook lasagna noodles really saves time and you don't have to worry about simmering a sauce all day or handling and tearing the hot noodles!

1 ½   pounds lean ground beef
1 tablespoon olive oil
1 medium onion; finely chopped
2 medium cloves garlic; minced
32 ounces ricotta cheese; part skim
2 large eggs
1 teaspoon basil leaves; dried
1 teaspoon oregano leaves; dried
1 tablespoon parsley flakes; dried
1 26-ounce jar spaghetti sauce; use your favorite!
1 15-ounce can tomato sauce
1 8-ounce pkg. No-cook lasagna noodles; use 12 noodles in all.
4 cups mozzarella cheese; shredded
1 cup Parmesan cheese; grated

Preheat oven to 350°.

Lightly grease bottom and sides of a deep 13x9-inch baking pan

Brown meat in a large, heavy skillet over medium heat; drain. Wipe pan clean and add olive oil and onions. Brown gently for 3 minutes, add garlic and continue cooking for 2 additional minutes. Reduce heat to low and stir in spaghetti sauce and tomato sauce.

In a medium-mixing bowl, combine the ricotta cheese, eggs, basil, oregano and parsley.

Spoon and spread 3/4 cup of meat sauce onto the bottom of your baking dish.

Place 3 no-cook lasagna noodles on top of the sauce. Top with 1 cup of sauce followed by 1/3 of the ricotta mixture. Place 3 more noodles, sauce and ricotta followed by 3 more noodles, sauce and ricotta. Place the reaming three noodles on top and spread the remaining sauce (it should be a thin layer) on top. Sprinkle the mozzarella and parmesan cheeses evenly over all.

• •

Cover with foil and bake 30 minutes (40 if straight from the refrigerator), uncover and bake another 15-20 minutes or until bubbly and lightly browned on top. Let stand about 10 minutes before cutting into squares.

Hint: Lay a large sheet of aluminum foil on the center rack of your oven and sit the lasagna on it; this will save the bottom of your oven from spillovers.

Stuffed Pasta with Tomato Cream Sauce

This simple sauce is wonderful and won't overpower the pasta. You can make the pasta yourself or purchase the fresh, meat-stuffed ravioli or tortellini at the grocery.

2 cups marinara sauce; homemade (see recipe index) or jarred
½ cup heavy cream
2 tablespoons fresh chopped basil (or 2 teaspoons dried)
½ cup grated Parmesan cheese
1 pound fresh ravioli or tortellini

In a large non-reactive saucepan, heat the marinara sauce over medium heat. Stir in cream and basil and heat together 2 to 3 minutes. Stir in 2 tablespoons of the cheese.

Cook the pasta in salted boiling water as directed on the package. Drain and pour into a large warm bowl.

Pour the sauce over the pasta and toss together. Pass the remaining Parmesan cheese on the side.

Homemade Lasagna

This is my own rendition of a very popular dish. It does take longer than my Lazy-Day version, but I think it tastes much better!

1 recipe Italian Meat Sauce (see recipe index)
3 large eggs
32 ounces ricotta cheese; part skim
1 ½ cup parmesan cheese
½ teaspoon basil leaves; dried
½ teaspoon oregano leaves; dried
¼ cup fresh parsley; chopped
1 teaspoon salt
¼ teaspoon pepper
2 pounds mozzarella cheese
1 pound lasagna noodles

Prepare the meat sauce and remove from heat.

In a large bowl, beat the eggs. Stir in the ricotta cheese, ½ cup Parmesan cheese, basil, oregano, parsley, salt and pepper. Mix with a wooden spoon until well blended.

Cook the lasagna noodles in a large pot of rapidly boiling salted water, stirring several times to prevent them from sticking together about 12 to 15 minutes. Drain in a colander and rinse well with cold running water, drain again.

To assemble lasagna, spread ¾ cup meat sauce (try to get limited meat in the sauce for this step) on the bottom of a large lasagna pan. Arrange a layer of noodles on the sauce. Spread 1 ½ cups sauce onto the noodles. Top with a layer of ½ ricotta cheese mixture and 1/3 cup Parmesan cheese. Repeat another layer of noodles, sauce, ricotta and Parmesan. End with a layer of noodles and sauce. Sprinkle remaining Parmesan cheese on sauce. (This recipe may be prepared to this up to a day ahead)

To bake, preheat oven to 350º. Cover with foil and bake 30 minutes (40 if straight from the refrigerator), uncover and bake another 15-20 minutes or until bubbly and lightly browned on top. Let stand about 10 minutes before cutting into squares. Serve with remaining sauce (warmed) on the side.

● ●

Fried Chicken with Biscuits, Baked Beans and Potato Salad (above)
Fried Fish with Hushpuppies, Cole Slaw and Grandaddy's Swamp Cabbage (below)

Traditional Barbequed Baby Back Ribs with English Pea Salad and Texas Toast

Holiday Ham (above)   *Mediterranean Salmon with Fettucine Romano (below)*

Al's Apple Cake (top right)   *Big Mama's Boiled Custard (left)*   *Pecan Pie (bottom right)*

Fettuccine with Classical Pesto Sauce

If you love basil, then Pesto sauce is for you! Try adding roasted vegetables to the pasta and the tossing in the pesto...yum!

2 cups packed fresh basil leaves
2 cloves garlic; minced
½ cup walnuts
1 ¼ cup extra-virgin olive oil
½ cup grated Parmesan cheese
½ cup grated Romano cheese
¾ teaspoon salt
1 pound fresh fettuccine (or boxed)
2 tablespoons butter

Place basil, garlic and walnuts into your food processor and process 15 seconds. With machine on, pour oil through the food shoot in a slow steady stream until almost 1 cup has been used. With machine still on, pour in the cheeses and then the remaining oil; process until smooth. Taste and season with salt, if needed.

Cook the fettuccini in boiling salt water until tender but still firm, about 2-3 minutes. Drain. Pour pasta into a large warm bowl and toss with the butter and 1 cup of pesto sauce. Pass the remaining pesto on the side.

Linguini with Clam Sauce – White or Red!

My husband loves red clam sauce while I prefer mine white! Therefore I have included both recipes to suit everyone! Prepare both sauces using directions below, serve over hot linguine and generously sprinkle with Parmesan Cheese.

Red Clam Sauce

2 Tbsp. good olive oil
2 Tbsp. butter
7 cloves garlic, minced
½ cup chopped fresh basil or 1 tablespoon dried
2 tsp. Oregano
½ tsp. Crushed red pepper
2 8-oz. bottles clam juice
1 29-oz. can diced tomatoes
1 8-oz. can tomato sauce
¾ cup white wine
1 cup water
3 6.5-oz. cans chopped clams
1 pound linguini; cooked and drained
shredded parmesan cheese

White Clam Sauce

2 Tbsp. good olive oil
2 Tbsp. butter
7 cloves garlic, minced
1 cup chopped fresh basil or 2 tablespoons dried
2 tsp. dried Oregano leaves
2 8-oz. bottles clam juice
¾ cup white wine
1 ½ cups water
cans chopped clams
1 pound linguini; cooked and drained
shredded parmesan cheese

Open all cans and drain the liquid from each can, together, into a large measuring cup; add the clam juice, tomato sauce (red sauce only), water and wine.

Heat the olive oil and the butter, over medium heat, in a large skillet.

Add garlic and gently sauté being careful not to over brown, about 1 minute. Add the basil, oregano, red pepper (red sauce only) and tomatoes (red sauce only) and cook together about 30 seconds.

Add the combined liquids. Simmer over medium heat for 10-15 minutes allowing the liquid to cook down by about 1 cup.

Add the clams, cover with glass lid and simmer for 1 minute. Serve over the hot, cooked linguini and pass the Parmesan cheese on the side.

Food Styling Tip

To make this dish more attractive to guests, use fresh clams in their shells; even if you just use a few for each serving along with the canned clams! Scrub the shells well and discard any that are open before cooking. You will need to use and additional bottle of clam sauce to make up for the lost canned liquid. Add the clams at the end, as directed in the recipe, and cook until they have all opened. Arrange the clams over the linguini and pour the sauce over all. Sprinkle fresh chopped parsley over all!

Baked Rigatoni

This is a hearty casserole-type dish that will serve a large crowd. You can always separate it into two pans and freeze one unbaked. You do not have to use rigatoni as ziti or penne will work just fine.

Italian Meat Sauce (see recipe index)

1 ½ pound rigatoni, Ziti or Penne pasta
1 pound mozzarella cheese; shredded
1 ½ cups Parmesan cheese; grated

Cook the pasta according to directions and drain.

Preheat oven to 350°. Ina large bowl, toss the pasta with 2/3 of the meat sauce. Stir in the mozzarella cheese and 1 cup Parmesan.

Pour pasta into a greased 9x13-inch pan.

Cover with remaining sauce and Parmesan cheese. Cover with foil and bake 25 minutes.

Uncover and bake another 10 minutes or until bubbly and lightly browned on top.

Gravies & Sauces

Entrees and Snacks
Are tasty and fine,
But give them a Sauce
And they're divine!

Tomato Gravy

A Southern Specialty and one of my Family's favorites!

3 slices bacon
1 onion; chopped
1 tablespoon flour
1 14.5-oz. can chopped tomatoes
pinch of sugar

Fry the bacon until crisp in a medium skillet. Drain and chop. Add the onion to the drippings and fry until they are soft and beginning to brown. Add the flour to the onion and stir well. Add in the tomatoes and the sugar and bring to a gentle boil. Add chopped bacon to the pan. Reduce heat and cook until ready to serve.

Serve over white rice.

Country-Style Cream Gravy

This is the gravy to serve with Country Fried Steak. You can also double this recipe and add ½ pound browned and drained sausage crumbles to serve over biscuits.

2 tablespoons butter (or drippings from pan)
2 tablespoons flour
1 cup milk (or half milk and half chicken broth)
¼ teaspoon salt
½ teaspoon coarse ground black pepper
½ teaspoon Worcestershire sauce

Melt the butter in skillet or saucepan over medium heat. Stir in the flour and cook about 1 minute or until flour just begins to brown. Slowly stir in milk, salt, pepper and Worcestershire sauce. Simmer and stir the gravy with a whisk until it begins to thicken and bubble.

Pan Gravy for Meats and Poultry

Making good gravy to serve with your meats and poultry does not have to be a dreaded experience! Start with the drippings and add the seasoning you like best. If the mixture becomes lumpy, simple pour it through a sieve and use a spoon to press the liquid through.

For Meat

2 tablespoons pan drippings
1-2 tablespoons flour
1 cup of degreased pan juices, water, wine, broth, cream, milk or a combination
salt and pepper
kitchen bouquet

Remove the meat from the pan and pour off all but 2 tablespoons of the drippings.
Blend 1-2 tablespoons flour into the drippings. Stir with a whisk until the mixture is well combined and smooth. Continue to cook and stir while adding 1 cup of liquid. Season the gravy with salt and pepper and add a few drops of kitchen bouquet until a rich color is achieved. Strain the gravy as needed and reheat before serving.

For Poultry

¼ cup of the fat
¼ cup flour
2 cups liquid; pan juices and enough broth to make 2 cups
¼ cup cream
salt and pepper

Strain the liquid from the roasted fowl. Separate the fat from the juices; save ½ cup fat and all of the juice. Heat the fat in a sauce pan. Add the flour and stir well until completely blended. Slowly stir in the 2 cups liquid. Simmer 5 minutes and then slowly add in the cream until heated through. Strain through a sieve if necessary, season to taste and serve.

Mushroom Wine Gravy

This is a simple variation of the pan gravy for meat, but boy does it make it great!

2 tablespoons butter
½ pound fresh mushrooms; sliced
3 green onions; thinly sliced
2 tablespoons pan drippings
1-2 tablespoons flour
½ cup of degreased pan juices
½ cup beef broth
¼ cup red wine
salt and pepper
kitchen bouquet

In medium skillet, sauté the mushrooms and onions in the butter for 3-4 minutes or until softened. Remove from the pan and set aside.

Add 2 tablespoons of meat drippings to the pan. Blend 1-2 tablespoons flour into the drippings. Stir with a whisk until the mixture is well combined and smooth. Continue to cook and stir while adding first the wine, then the pan juices and broth. Season the gravy with salt and pepper and add a few drops of kitchen bouquet until a rich color is achieved. Return the mushroom and onions to the pan and simmer 5 minutes.

Sweet and Sour Sauce – Luau Style

This is a Polynesian version for luau-type foods such as meatballs. You can also add it to vegetable and meat stir-fries!

2 tablespoons cornstarch
½ cup chicken broth
2 tablespoons soy sauce
2 tablespoons butter
1 cup chicken broth
¾ -1 cup green peppers; diced
6 slices canned pineapple rings; diced
¾ cup pineapple juice
½ cup mild vinegar
¼ cup brown sugar
¼ cup granulated sugar
½ teaspoon salt
¼ teaspoon ginger

Make a paste of the cornstarch, ½ cup broth and soy sauce.

In a heavy pan, melt the butter over medium heat. Add the green peppers and cook 2 minutes.

Add in the chicken broth and pineapple, cover and simmer 5 minutes. While mixture is bubbly, add the cornstarch paste and the remaining ingredients.

Simmer, stirring often until the mixture thickens.

Barbeque Sauce

This is a good basic barbeque sauce for grilling or dipping! It is a bit on the sweet side so if you like a spicier sauce, cut back on the sugar!

2 cups ketchup
½ cup vinegar
¼ cup brown sugar
¼ cup granulated
¼ teaspoon garlic salt
¼ teaspoon onion salt
¼ teaspoon celery salt
3 teaspoons Liquid Smoke
½ cup Worcestershire sauce

Heat all ingredients to a simmer in a large saucepan until sugars are melted. Cover, reduce heat and cook slowly for 30 minutes. Serve hot, use for cooking or store in the refrigerator for later use.

Gingered Balsamic Vinegar Sauce

This is excellent on grilled or broiled salmon or other hearty fish!

¼ cup balsamic vinegar
1 tablespoon fresh ginger; grated
1 tablespoon minced green onion
1 clove garlic; minced

Bring all ingredients to a simmer in a small non-reactive skillet. Simmer 5 minutes, remove from heat and pour over grilled fish.

Seafood Sauce

This is a great sauce to serve with crab cakes, fish or any time you want an alternative to tartar sauce.

1 cup mayonnaise
¼ cup ketchup
¼ cup chili sauce
2 tablespoon vegetable oil
1 clove garlic
½ small onion
1 tablespoon vinegar
½ cup parsley
½ teaspoon dry mustard
¼ teaspoon paprika
1 tsp. Worcestershire sauce
Juice of ½ lemon
Dash Tabasco sauce

Place all ingredients together in a blender. Blend until creamy. Refrigerate until ready to serve.

Tartar Sauce

You can easily make this with your food processor! Use with fish, on fish sandwiches or with crab cakes.

1 Cups Mayonnaise
1 ¼ teaspoon lemon juice
4-5 large sweet gherkin pickles
1 teaspoon sweet gherkin pickle juice
½ teaspoon prepared yellow mustard
¼ small onion

Place all ingredients into a food processor. Process on the lowest speed using the pulse button until the pickles and onions are into small bits the mixture is smooth. Chill before using.

Cocktail Sauce

I love a lot of horseradish in my cocktail sauce! If you are used to bottled sauce or are not so fond of a spicy cocktail, add the horseradish, a little at a time, until the flavor you like is achieved!

1 cup ketchup
juice from ½ lemon
1 Tbsp. prepared horseradish; or to taste
2 tsp. Worcestershire sauce
½ tsp. salt
dash Tabasco sauce

Mix all ingredients together. Chill before serving with cold or hot boiled shrimp.

Hollandaise Sauce

I often make this on HSN using my blender or immersion blender. It is wonderful on fresh steamed vegetables like asparagus and broccoli and is a must have on your Eggs Benedict!

3 egg yolks
2 Tbsp. lemon juice
¼ tsp. salt
¼ tsp. cayenne pepper
½ cup hot, melted butter

Combine egg yolks, lemon juice, salt and cayenne pepper in your blender (or in a beaker if using an immersion blender). Cover and pulse several times. Remove the measuring cap on the lid, switch blender to high speed and gradually add the melted butter in a steady stream, until just blended and thickened. Serve immediately. Makes 1 cup sauce.

Horseradish Dill Sauce

I love this sauce on roasted beef, salmon steaks and boiled red potatoes. It tastes gourmet but is simple to make...especially if you are using your hand mixer!

¼ cup prepared horseradish
1 cup sour cream
¼ cup fresh dill weed; chopped
1 tsp. lemon juice
¼ tsp. salt
¼ cup whipping cream

Mix together the horseradish, sour cream, dill, lemon juice and salt. Use the whisk attachment of your hand mixer and whip the cream until thick. Stir into the horseradish mixture.

Variation: If you do not like the flavor of dill, use green onions instead!

Mint Pesto Sauce

Delicious on lamb!

1 cup packed fresh mint leaves
½ cup fresh parsley leaves
¼ cup walnuts
3 cloves garlic
1 cup plus 2 tablespoons extra-virgin olive oil
2 tablespoons white wine vinegar
1 ¾ teaspoons salt
½ teaspoon pepper

Place the mint, parsley, walnuts and garlic into a food processor and chop. With the machine on, slowly pour in 1 cup of the olive oil and continue to process until mixture is very finely chopped but not pureed. Season with the vinegar, ¾ teaspoon salt and ¼ teaspoon pepper.

● ●

Cheese Sauce

This is a good, basic cheese sauce to pour over steamed vegetables, omelets or anything that needs a little dressing up!

2 tablespoons butter
2 tablespoons flour
1 cup milk or cream
1 cup grated cheese (any variety you like)
½ teaspoon salt
1/8 teaspoon paprika

In a medium saucepan, melt butter over medium heat. Stir in flour until smooth and creamy. Slowly whisk or stir in the milk until smooth and hot. Reduce heat and add the cheese, salt and paprika. Slowly cook until the cheese has melted and the sauce is creamy.

Use as desired.

Food Styling Tip

Whenever you are pouring a 1- color sauce over foods, always top it with a spice or ingredient of a different color. For example, if you are pouring cheese sauce over a ham omelet, sprinkle chopped ham on top. If it is going over nachos, add a little cayenne pepper or jalapenos and if it is going over a vegetable add a little paprika, black pepper or parsley!

Vegetables & Sides

An entrée alone
Won't fill up the plate,
So whip up a Side Dish
To make dinner great!

Italian Vegetable Bake

This is a great tasting dish that is light but filling. Use whatever vegetables you like that are fresh in your produce section. Below are my favorites!

1 tablespoon olive oil
½ medium white onion; very coarsely chopped
1 yellow pepper; very coarsely chopped
½ pound fresh mushrooms; sliced
2 medium-small zucchini; sliced thin
10 cherry tomatoes; halved
1 tablespoon Italian Seasoning
¼ cup Parmesan cheese
2 tablespoons dried seasoned breadcrumbs
2 tablespoons butter

Preheat oven to 350°.

Heat the oil, in a large skillet, over medium heat and sauté the onions with the peppers for 1-2 minutes. Remove from pan and set aside. Add mushrooms to the pan and cook quickly for 2 minutes, stirring constantly. Return onions and peppers to the pan, add the zucchini and cook another 2-3 minutes. Add the tomatoes and the seasoning; stir well.

Pour the mixture into an 8x8-inch baking pan. Sprinkle on cheese and breadcrumbs and dot with butter. Bake for 20 minutes or until bubbly and top is lightly browned.

Cheesy Garlic Smashed Potatoes

I love mashed potatoes! This version is called "smashed" because I leave on some of the peelings. I really like the addition of the cheese and garlic but if you prefer traditional mashed potatoes just peel all of the potatoes and omit the garlic and cheese!

10 medium white potatoes; peel half of the potatoes and cut them all in quarters
3 cloves garlic, peeled whole
3 tsp. salt
1 tsp. coarse-ground black pepper
½ stick butter, melted
¾ cup half-and-half, warmed
1 cup shredded sharp cheddar

Halved the potatoes and place them into a large saucepan or Dutch oven with the garlic and 2 tsp. salt. Just cover with warm water.

Bring to a boil and cook, uncovered 12-15 minutes or until potatoes are fork tender. Drain potatoes, reserving 2 tablespoons of the liquid.

Place cooked potatoes into a medium-mixing bowl and add the salt, pepper, butter, reserved liquid and the ½ cup of half-and-half.

Using the medium speed of your hand mixer, whip to desired consistency adding more half-and-half if needed. Add cheese and mix in on lowest speed until blended Adjust salt and pepper to taste.

Food Styling Tip

Save some of the cheese to sprinkle on the top before serving. You may also top with fresh chopped parsley. If you were to make this for camera, you would not use black pepper that would look spotty, you would use white pepper instead!

Scalloped Potatoes (Plain or Fancy)

Scalloped potatoes are a great side dish or can be made into a main meal by adding some tidbits or leftovers!

3 cups potatoes; peeled and sliced thinly
6 cups rapidly boiling water
1 tsp. salt
2 Tbsp. flour
6 Tbsp. butter
1 ¼ cup half 'n half
1 ¼ tsp. salt
¼ tsp. paprika
¼ tsp. dry mustard

Use the thin slicing blade of your Bravetti 600-Watt Platinum-Pro Food Processor to thinly slice your peeled potatoes until you have about 3 cups. Drop potato slices into boiling water with 1 tsp. salt. Parboil for 8 minutes. Drain well.

Grease a 10" baking dish and place 1 layer of potatoes on the bottom. Sprinkle with some of the flour and dab with some of the butter. Continue this until all potatoes, flour and butter have been used.

In a small pan, heat half 'n half and spices, or, you may use a glass bowl and cook in the microwave about 1 ½ minutes. Pour mixture over the potatoes and cook at 350° for about 35 minutes or until the top is golden brown and bubbly.

Variations: You may add to the layers ¼ chopped green onions or chives, ¼ sweet red peppers, ½ cup mushrooms, 3 slices minced crisp bacon, ¼ cup small ham cubes, ¼ cup finely chopped broccoli florets or 1/3 cup of your favorite shredded cheese. I do suggest slightly cooking the vegetables before adding to the layers and increasing the pan size if you add more than one addition

Creamed Spinach

I love creamed spinach. To me, it is the ultimate comfort food...plus, it's good for me! It's good for you, too!

10 oz. frozen spinach; thawed and patted dry
3 Tbs. soft butter
1 clove garlic; very finely minced
½ small white onion; very finely minced
2 Tbs. flour
¾ cup milk
½ tsp. salt
¼ tsp. paprika
¼ tsp. dry mustard
¼ cup grated Parmesan cheese
¼ cup seasoned breadcrumbs
4 Tbs. butter; cut into small pieces

Preheat oven to 350°.

Process spinach, in your food processor, until almost pureed. Place in fine colander and squeeze out any remaining liquid; set aside.

In a skillet, over medium heat, melt the butter along with the minced garlic and onion; stir constantly until butter is completely melted and bubbly. Stir in flour until blended. Slowly add flour stirring constantly. Add salt and paprika and allow mixture to come to a gentle boil. When the sauce is hot and smooth, stir in spinach and cook 3 minutes.

You may serve the spinach now or, transfer to a greased 8" baking dish and evenly sprinkle top with Parmesan cheese, breadcrumbs and butter pieces. Bake for 15 minutes or until bubbly.

Zucchini-Tomato Cheese Bake

My daughter, Merritt, loves this dish and asked me to put this in the book so she could make it herself. Here you go sweetie!

2 tablespoons olive oil
2 cloves garlic; minced
3 medium zucchini; sliced into ½-inch thick rounds
1 14.5-oz. can diced tomatoes; drained
1 tablespoon Italian Seasoning
½ teaspoon salt
1 ½ cups mozzarella cheese; shredded
¼ cup grated Parmesan cheese
2 tablespoons seasoned breadcrumbs

Preheat oven to 350°.

Heat the oil in a large skillet over medium heat. Add the garlic and stir quickly for 1 minute. Add the zucchini and cook 2-3 minutes or until they start to soften. Add in the tomatoes, Italian seasoning, salt and 1 cup of the mozzarella cheese; toss well.

Lightly grease a 8x8-inch pan. Pour the mixture in the pan. Combine remaining ½ cup mozzarella cheese, the Parmesan cheese and the breadcrumbs and sprinkle evenly on the top.

Bake 20-25 minutes or until the mixture is bubbly and the top is lightly browned.

Oven-Roasted Potatoes

A delicious alternative to a baked potato!

10 small red new potatoes; quartered
¼ cup extra-virgin olive oil
¼ cup grated Parmesan cheese
1 Tbsp. dried parsley
½ tsp. salt
¼ tsp. paprika

Preheat oven to 400°. Put all ingredients into a zip-close baggie.
Toss well. Place coated potatoes in a single layer on a non-stick
jellyroll pan. Bake for 20 minutes or until crispy outside and fork
tender inside.

Red Cabbage and Apples

This is a great side dish to serve with pork or grilled sausages.

3 tablespoons bacon drippings
4 cups red cabbage; shredded
2 cups apples; unpeeled but cubed
¼ cup brown sugar
¼ cup vinegar
1 ¼ teaspoons salt
pepper to taste
¼ cup water

In a large skillet, heat bacon drippings over medium. Add cabbage,
apples, sugar, vinegar, salt and pepper. Add water and cover tightly
to steam for 5-7 minutes. Uncover and simmer until cabbage and
apples are cooked but still crisp.

Asparagus Bundles

Asparagus is great anyway you cook it, but the bacon really dresses it up and makes a nice presentation for a dinner party. If you don't want to serve it bundled, just increase cooking time by 4 minutes and serve as is or with hollandaise sauce!

1 tablespoon olive oil
1 tablespoon butter
1 clove garlic; minced
juice from ½ lemon
½ cup water
¼ cup dry white wine
½ teaspoon salt
¼ teaspoon pepper
1 lb. medium asparagus; woody ends removed
2 strips of bacon

Preheat oven to 375°.

Heat the olive oil and the butter over medium heat in a large skillet. Add garlic and sauté for 1 minute. Add the lemon, water, wine, salt and pepper. Bring to a rapid boil. Add the asparagus to the liquid and return to a boil. Cover, reduce heat and simmer 5-6 minutes or until asparagus is barely tender.

Divide the asparagus into 4 bundles and wrap each bundle with ½ strip bacon. Place on a shallow baking pan and bake for 10 minutes or until bacon is brown and crisping.

Food Styling Tip

Wrap the asparagus tips with aluminum foil to prevent them from over-browning. If you do not want to use bacon, slice red peppers into rings and slide the bundles through the ring.

Cauliflower or Broccoli Au Gratin

This dish is so good, even the kids will eat their veggies!

1 large head cauliflower; cut into flowerets
1 ½ cups water
½ tsp. salt
6 Tbsp. butter
4 Tbsp. flour
½ tsp. salt
¼ tsp pepper
¼ tsp. onion powder
¼ tsp. dry mustard
2 cups cold milk
1 cup sharp cheddar cheese
4 Tbsp. minced parsley
Cornflakes; crumbled
Paprika

Bring the cauliflower, 1 ½ cups water and ½ tsp. salt to a full boil. Cook for 5 minutes if using cauliflower and 3 minutes if using broccoli. Pour into a colander and drain.

In a small saucepan, blend butter, flour, salt, pepper, onion powder and dry mustard together over medium heat. Add cold milk and cook slowly, stirring frequently until a smooth sauce is achieved. Add the cheese and parsley; cook until cheese is melted.

Pour a small amount of sauce into a lightly greased casserole dish; then add a layer of cauliflower or broccoli. Continue, alternating layers of sauce and vegetable, making the last layer sauce.

Crumble a small amount of cornflakes and sprinkle over the top. Shake paprika over all and bake 20 to 30 minutes in a 375° oven.

Macaroni & Cheese

Everyone loves macaroni and cheese so feel free to double the recipe and bake in a larger dish!

8 oz. elbow macaroni
1 cup sharp cheddar cheese; shredded
1 cup Monterey Jack cheese; shredded
2 Tbsp. grated onion
½ tsp. salt
1/8 tsp. cayenne pepper
¼ tsp. dry mustard
1 1/3 cups milk
2 eggs; beaten
½ cup dry breadcrumbs
2 Tbs. butter
Paprika

Boil macaroni according to the package directions. Blanch in cold water to prevent sticking. Lightly butter a 8x8-inch baking dish. Layer into the dish, starting with the macaroni, alternate layers of macaroni and the shredded cheese; ending with cheese on top.

Beat the onion, salt, cayenne pepper, dry mustard, milk and eggs together until well blended. Pour this mixture over the macaroni. Sprinkle breadcrumbs evenly on top and dot with the butter; lightly sprinkle paprika over all.

Bake in a 350° oven for about 30-40 minutes or until bubbly and lightly browned on top.

Food Styling Tip

When applying the breadcrumbs to the top, leave about 2-inches around the edge plain. Before serving, lightly sprinkle the breadcrumbs with sliced green onion leaves, chopped parsley or chopped tomato.

Amazing Artichokes

If you love artichokes then you'll love this recipe. I always make mine in the pressure cooker because they cook so much faster. If you do not have a pressure cooker, follow the directions below, but use a large saucepan and cook the artichokes for 25-35 minutes.

4 medium-large artichokes
1 ½ cups water
½ stick butter
½ tsp. salt
3 cloves garlic minced
1 lemon
¼ cup white wine

Prepare artichokes by cutting the top down flat (about 1 to 2 inches), snipping points off the remaining leaves and trimming the stem flush with the bottom. Set aside. Prepare lemon by cutting it into half; squeeze one half and cut the other into thin rings.

In your Pressure Cooker, heat butter over medium. Add garlic and toss for 1 minute. Add the wine and lemon juice. Stir. Add the salt, water and lemon slices. Place the artichokes; flat tops down/bottoms up, into the liquid.

Attach the pressure lid and select the highest pressure setting. When full pressure is reached, lower heat the medium-low and cook for 10 minutes. Remove pan from heat and use cold water to quickly release the pressure.

Serve hot with a dollop of homemade Mayonnaise (see recipe index).

Southern Style Green Beans and New Potatoes

My Grandfather always had a very large garden so we started by picking the beans ourselves! Then my Grandmother, Mom and myself would sit on the porch and snap the beans and then cook them, along with small red potatoes, in this manner.

2 large handfuls (about 2 pounds) fresh green beans
8 very small red potatoes; scrubbed
1 ham hock
1 small onion; peeled
1 cube beef or vegetable bullion
¼ teaspoon salt
¼ teaspoon coarse black pepper

Remove the ends from the beans and snap them in half; wash and drain. Put the beans and the scrubbed potatoes into a large saucepan or Dutch oven. Cover 2-inches over the top of the beans and potatoes with cold water. Bring to a boil over medium-high heat.

Add the ham hock, whole onion, bullion cube, salt and pepper. Return to a boil , cover, reduce heat and cook 25-30 minutes or until the potatoes are fork tender. Taste and season with additional salt and pepper if needed.

Food Styling Tip

For a decorative effect, peel all but a thin ring of skin, in the middle, from the potatoes. Then, instead of adding the potatoes and beans to the cold-water get the water boiling, add the other ingredients and let simmer 30 minutes to flavor the water. Add the potatoes and cook 12-15 minutes, then add the beans and cook just 8 minutes. They won't taste near as good, but the color will stay pretty!

Elizabeth's Green Beans

Elizabeth Watts, my friend and a great demonstrator for the Euro-Pro products on HSN, gave me this delicious recipe for green beans. I always see her cleaning on HSN but now I know she can cook too!

1 pound fresh, long thin green beans; ends trimmed
1 tablespoon butter
1 tablespoons olive oil
2 shallots; sliced into thin rounds
1 tablespoon Balsamic vinegar
¼ cup parmesan cheese; shredded
salt and fresh ground pepper to taste

Bring 1-inch water to a rapid boil in a medium saucepan. Add beans, toss, cover, reduce heat and steam for 6-8 minutes or until beans are tender but still firm. Drain.

In a small skillet, heat the butter and olive oil over medium heat. Add the shallots and, stirring frequently, cook 2-3 minutes or until they are soft. Add in the balsamic vinegar and cook another 1-2 minutes until they look caramelized and most of the vinegar is cooked away.

Place the beans into a warm serving bowl. Add the shallots and the cheese and toss to coat. Season with salt and fresh ground black pepper to taste.

Yellow Crookneck Squash Casserole

I love this buttery squash casserole. We often had it as part of our family get-together food spread.

2 slices bacon
4-5 large yellow squash, cut into ½-inch disks
1 medium onion; cut in ½-inch thick half-rounds
½ teaspoon salt
¼ teaspoon pepper
2 tablespoons grated Parmesan cheese
3 tablespoons dried breadcrumbs
1 tablespoon butter

Preheat oven to 350°.

Cook the bacon until crisp in a heavy skillet or cast iron fry pan. Remove bacon, drain, chop and set aside.

Heat the drippings over medium heat. Add onions and fry 2-3 minutes until onions are soft. Add the squash and cook another 2 minutes. Remove from heat, add the Parmesan cheese, chopped bacon, salt and pepper and toss together.

Lightly grease a 8x8-inch baking pan. Pour squash mixture into the pan. Sprinkle on the breadcrumbs and dot with butter. Bake for 20-25 minutes until the top is lightly browned.

Food Styling Tip

Save some of the bacon crumbles and add to the top of the casserole during the last 5-8 minutes of cooking!

Baked Beans

I have always received complements on my baked beans. I hope you like them as well!

1 53-oz. can Pork and Beans
1 medium onion
1 tablespoon prepared yellow mustard
2 tablespoons packed brown sugar
2 tablespoons ketchup
2 tablespoon Worcestershire sauce
1 teaspoon cider vinegar
½ teaspoon salt
½ teaspoon liquid smoke
2 pieces bacon; cut in half

Preheat oven to 375°.

Cut both ends off the onion and peel. Starting at the large end, cut 4 thin slices; set aside. Finely chop the remaining of the onion.

In a large mixing bowl, stir together the beans, chopped onion, mustard, brown sugar, ketchup, Worcestershire sauce, vinegar, salt and liquid smoke.

Pour the mixture into a 8x8-inch baking dish. Place the 4 pieces of bacon on top of the beans. Separate the onion rings and scatter over the beans and bacon.

Bake for 35-45 minutes or until onion is brown and the beans are bubbly hot. Discard the bacon and top onions, if desired, before serving.

Lucky Black-Eyed Peas (Hoppin' John)

Traditionally, eating Black-Eyed peas on New Year's Day brings good luck in the coming year. I don't know if it's true or not, but I've never bucked the tradition and I've had a great life so far!

1 pound fresh or frozen black-eyed peas
6 cups water
1 cup onion; chopped
½ teaspoon pepper
1 bay leaf
½ teaspoon salt
1 small smoked ham hock
4-6 cups cooked white rice

In a large pot or Dutch oven, cover the beans with fresh water.

Add the onions, pepper, and bay leaf and return to a boil. Cover, reduce heat and simmer 15 minutes. Add ham hock and salt and simmer, uncovered, another 45 minutes to 1 hour or until the beans are tender.

Discard the ham hock and bay leaf.

Serve atop white rice and with hot, buttered Corn Bread (see recipe index).

Pass around chow-chow relish or chopped fresh onion and tomato.

Sweet Potato Casserole

You have to have this on your Thanksgiving table! Marshmallows are optional!

1 40-oz. can sweet potatoes (or 3 large sweet potatoes, peeled, boiled and drained)
2 cups milk
4 eggs; well beaten
8 tablespoons butter or margarine; melted
1 cup granulated sugar
½ cup light brown sugar; packed
¼ teaspoon ground cloves
½ teaspoon ground nutmeg
1 teaspoon ground cinnamon
crushed pineapple or miniature marshmallows (optional)

Preheat oven to 350°.

Drain the canned sweet potatoes. In a large bowl, mash the potatoes and add butter, milk, eggs, sugar and spices blending thoroughly. Pour the potato mixture into a lightly greased 9x13-inch baking dish.

Bake 30 to 45 minutes.

Optional: When the edges appear cooked, top with crushed pineapple and/or marshmallows and continue cooking until marshmallows are golden brown.

Food Styling Tip

Cut the top 1/3 off of 6 oranges and hollow them out; use a melon-baller to scrape clean. After the mixture has cooked in the pan for 15 minutes, remove from oven and scoop into the hollowed out oranges; mounding slightly. Top with marsh mellows and chopped pecans, if desired, and bake for 10 minutes.

Creamed Peas and Pearl Onions

An easy dish to make that seems fancy to guests!

9-10 small white pearl onions
1 ½ cups salted water
2 cups frozen peas; thawed
¼ cup butter
3 tablespoons flour
1 ½ cup half and half cream
2 tablespoons dry white wine
Dash cayenne pepper
Dash black pepper
½ teaspoon salt
¼ cup slivered almonds; toasted

Toast the almonds in a 350° oven until browned stirring once or twice to get both sides.

Bring water to boil in a small saucepan. Place onions into a medium saucepan and pour boiling water over them. After 5 minutes use a slotted spoon and take the onions out of the water and remove the outer skin. Place the peeled onions back into the water, bring to a boil and cook 8-10 minutes or until tender. Drain the onions reserving 2 tablespoons of the liquid.

In a small saucepan, melt the butter. Add in the flour and mix until smooth. Slowly stir in the cream and bring to a gentle boil. Add in the peas and return to a gentle boil. Stir in the reserved onion liquid, the white wine, salt and pepper. Add in the onions and heat through. Pour the mixture into a warmed serving bowl and sprinkle the toasted almonds on the top.

Bread Bites

A loaf of bread
May be boring and dull,
But buttery morsels
Are wonderful!

Hushpuppies

If you are having fried fish for dinner, you need to have hushpuppies with it! They are easy to make and add that Southern touch to any meal!

2 teaspoon salt
3 ½ teaspoons baking powder
3 tablespoons sugar
2 cups yellow corn meal
¼ cup flour
2 eggs; beaten well
1 1/3 cup milk
½ cup onion; very finely chopped (optional)
3-4 dashes Tabasco sauce

Sift together, in a medium mixing bowl, the salt, baking powder, sugar, cornmeal and flour. Beat the milk and eggs together and pour into dry ingredients. Add the onion and Tabasco and stir the mixture well. Let sit 5 minutes.

Shape into small balls or drop off the end of a teaspoon into deep hot fat (374°). Fry until golden brown.

Texas Toast

In Texas, they make this using square bread, you can substitute the square bread for thick slices of French bread if you must. This is also great grilled!

1 loaf unsliced bakery white bread or French Bread
1 stick butter
1 clove garlic; minced very fine
1 tablespoon dried parsley

Preheat oven to 400°.

Slice the bread into 1-inch thick slices and arrange on a large cookie or baking sheet.
Melt the butter with the garlic over medium-low heat. Reduce heat to low and allow to cook 2-3 minutes being careful not to brown the butter. Remove from heat and stir in parsley.

Use a basting brush and completely cover both sides of the bread with the butter. Place the pan into the hot oven and heat for 4-5 minutes. Turn the bread over and heat another 4-5 minutes until the bread is lightly browned on both sides but still soft.

Or heat on the grill for 2 minutes per side.

Cornbread

This is best made in a cast iron skillet if you have one! My cornbread is light and a little on the sweet side, so if you like your cornbread not-so-sweet reduce the sugar by 2-3 tablespoons.

¼ cup shortening or margarine
2 ¼ cups cornmeal; fine
1 cup flour
2 tablespoons baking powder
1 teaspoon salt
¼ cup sugar
2 large eggs
2 cups milk

Preheat oven to 425°.

Place the oil into a 9x9-inch baking pan or a medium cast iron skillet and place into the oven to heat for 3-4 minutes.

In a medium-mixing bowl, add cornmeal, flour, baking powder, salt and sugar. Mix well with a spoon until all the dry ingredients are blended together. Beat the eggs into the milk. Pour into dry ingredients and mix well.

Remove the pan from the oven and pour the oil, leaving enough in the pan just to coat, into the mixture. Mix well. Pour batter into the hot pan and bake 15-20 minutes or until the edges pull away from the pan and the top is very lightly browned.

Homemade Pretzels

My husband Al loves soft pretzels. He buys the frozen ones that you microwave but always complains that they aren't near as good as the ones he gets up north or at the gourmet pretzel places. So, one day I decided to make them at home...he absolutely loved them! Word to the wise...make a lot!

1 envelope yeast, rapid rise
1 1/4 cups warm water
2 teaspoons sugar
2 teaspoons salt
4 cups all-purpose flour
butter as needed
8 teaspoons baking soda
coarse salt for sprinkling

Dissolve the yeast in 1/4 cup water in large mixing bowl. Then stir in the additional cup of warm water, the sugar and the salt.

Beat in the flour to make a stiff dough; add additional flour as needed. Knead the dough until it is elastic. Return to mixing bowl, gently rub with butter until lightly coated. Cover bowl with a towel, place in a warm, draft-free place and allow to rise for 45 minutes of until the dough has doubled in size.

Roll the dough into a rectangle about 8 inches wide and 20 inches long. Use a pizza cutter to cut into 14 long strips. Shape as desired.

Bring 8 cups of water to a boil with the baking soda. Drop in the pretzels 3 at a time. Boil for about 1 minute or until they float to the top. Remove and drain on a clean kitchen towel. Place on a buttered cookie sheet and sprinkle with salt.

Bake the pretzels for 14 minutes, or until golden brown, in a 475 oven.

● ●

Corn Fritters

These are good to serve in place of hushpuppies or with a hot bowl of soup or chili!

1 egg
½ cup milk
1 12-oz. can whole kernel corn; drained
1 tablespoon vegetable oil
1 cup flour
1 tablespoon sugar
½ teaspoon salt
1 teaspoon baking powder

In a medium mixing bowl, beat the egg with the milk. Add in the corn and the oil; mix. Sift together the dry ingredients and add them to the egg mixture. Stir just enough to mix.

Drop by the spoonful into hot deep oil (385°) and fry until golden brown.

Popovers and Yorkshire Pudding

Popovers are like bread cupcakes with nothing but air in the center!
They are derived from the British Yorkshire Puddings, where they
use the dripping from a beef roast instead of shortening. I love
them both! If they pop-up in not-so-perfect shapes...don't worry, it
adds a little character to your meal and they still taste great!

Shortening or the drippings from a beef roast
¾ cup milk
¼ cup water
3 eggs
1 cup flour
½ teaspoon salt

Preheat oven to 375°.

Use a hand mixer or blender and beat together the milk, water and
eggs. Add in the flour and salt and mix until smooth.

Put a little shortening into 12 muffin cups (use a 12-muffin tin or
individual tins). Place into the oven until melted and hot; 3-4
minutes.

Remove the hot tins from the oven and pour equal amounts of
batter into each cup. Return to the oven and bake 15-20 minute or
until puffed and golden brown.

Dinner Rolls

This is a great make-ahead dinner roll recipe that I learned from Polly Clingerman a few years ago. I like it because I can make the dough early and store it in the refrigerator until I am ready to bake my rolls...it even keeps overnight!

2 packages yeast
1/3 cup very warm water
2 cups milk
5 tablespoons sugar
½ cut butter or margarine
2 eggs; slightly beaten
1 teaspoon salt
6-7 cups flour

Combine the yeast, warm water and 1 tablespoon sugar in a large mixing bowl; let stand until foamy.

In a small saucepan, over medium heat, warm the milk with the remaining sugar, salt and butter until butter has melted. Remove from heat and cool 5 minutes. Pour the milk mixture into the yeast mixture. Slightly beat the eggs and add to the mixing bowl.

Use the dough hooks and the lowest speed of your Bravetti hand mixer, or a wooden spoon, and beat in the flour, one cup at the time, until a soft dough has formed.

Place the dough into a large, greased container, cover and let rise in a warm, draft-free place, until doubled in size. Punch down the dough and place it in the refrigerator for 3-4 hours or overnight.

Divide into 24 pieces, shape into balls or knots and place on a greased cookie sheet and let rise until double (about 30 minutes). Bake at 400° for 18 to 20 minutes.

Food Styling Tip

Let the dough balls rise and bake in the wells of a muffin tin if you want perfect shaped rolls!

Sweet Treats

I love lunch
And dinner too,
But sometimes only
Sweets will do!

Fruit Cocktail Cake

Carol, a very sweet and wonderful lady who happens to be my Step-Mother-In-Law (and very good cook!), gave me this recipe to share with everyone!

Cake

2 cups flour
1 ½ cup white sugar
2 teaspoons baking soda
2 large eggs; lightly beaten
1 15-oz. can fruit cocktail with juice
1 cup brown sugar
1 cup walnuts; chopped

Topping

1 stick margarine
½ cup white sugar
1 6-oz. can milk
1 tablespoon vanilla

Cool Whip or Whipped Cream (optional)

Preheat oven to 350°. Grease and flour a 9x13-inch baking pan.

Mix flour, sugar and baking soda together. Add eggs and fruit cocktail; mix and pour into prepared pan. Mix together the brown sugar and walnuts and sprinkle over the cake batter. Bake for 45 minutes.

Ten minutes before cake is done, melt the margarine in a small saucepan. Add sugar, canned milk and vanilla; stir until dissolved. Spoon hot liquid over the cake immediately after removing it from the oven.

Allow cake to cool and serve with a whipped topping if desired.

Everything Cookies

These are the cookies I always make on HSN to demonstrate the power of the Bravetti Hand Mixers! They taste so good, people place dibs on the dough to take home and bake with their families! I usually give it to my good friend Carol Graff; she is a very talented Food Stylist at HSN and gives me invaluable help!

1 cup light brown sugar (firmly packed)
1 cup granulated sugar
4 sticks of butter or margarine
4 large eggs
1 ½ tsp. vanilla
4 ½ cups all-purpose flour
1 tablespoon baking soda
1 tablespoon baking powder
1 cup chocolate chips
1 cup peanut butter candies or M&M's
1 cup coarsely chopped walnuts

In a large bowl, beat the sugars, butter, eggs and vanilla until creamy using your hand mixer. Switch mixer to low speed and add the flour, baking soda and baking powder and mix until cookie dough is smooth. Remove beaters and insert dough hooks. Add the candy, chips and nuts; blend just until mixed.

Drop rounded teaspoons of dough onto an un-greased cookie sheet. Bake at 375° for
8-10 minutes or until light golden brown. Let cool on cookie sheet for 5 minutes and then transfer to a cooling rack. Store cookies in an airtight container.

Food Styling Tip

To make these as great looking as they taste, set aside about 1/3 of the chocolate chips, candies and walnuts. After the dough is in place on the cookie sheet, push down gently to form a slightly flattened surface. Set a few of the extra candies, chips and nuts evenly onto each of the flattened surface; that way each cookie will look loaded with goodies!

● ●

Pumpkin Cheesecake

I always make this delicious dessert when demonstrating my pressure cooker on HSN. It cooks much faster and tastes great. If you do not have a pressure cooker, follow the alternative directions below.

1 cup cinnamon graham cracker crumbs
½ cup granulated sugar
½ stick butter, melted
16 oz. cream cheese, softened
1 Tbsp. butter
1 tsp. vanilla
1 cup brown sugar, firmly packed
1 can (16 oz.) solid-pack pumpkin
2 Tbs. cornstarch
1 tsp. cinnamon
¾ tsp. nutmeg
3 large eggs
2 cups hot water

Generously butter bottom and sides of 8" spring form pan. Sprinkle graham cracker crumbs and sugar evenly on bottom of pan; drizzle butter overall. Set pan aside.

In large mixing bowl, use your hand mixer to mix together cream cheese, vanilla and butter. Add next 5 ingredients and continue mixing. Mix in 1 egg at a time until smooth. Pour into pan.

Cover top with wax paper and then completely cover entire pan with aluminum foil crimping top and bottom edges to seal out moisture. Place riser in bottom of 8 qt. Pan of your Bravetti Platinum-Pro Pressure Cooker; add the hot water. Lower cake pan into pot and set atop riser. Attach lid, bring to full pressure (III), reduce heat and cook 45 minutes. Slowly release pressure, remove pan, uncover and refrigerate at least 3 hours.

Remove the side of the spring form pan. Slice and top with Spiced Whipped Topping.

Hint: Make a sling out of an aluminum foil strip (about 24" long and doubled for strength) to place under the spring form pan to aid in removal of hot pan.

Variation: If you are not using a pressure cooker follow the directions above except: After you pour it into the pan, place the pan on the center rack of a 300° oven. Place a shallow pan of water on the lower rack directly below the cake. Cook 1 ¼ hour. Place on a wire rack to cool and set or, turn oven off and allow it to set in the oven another hour to cool and set. Refrigerate, remove sides of spring form pan, slice and serve!

Jill's Key Lime Pie

My absolute favorite pie is even better now that I got my good friend Jill's recipe. Of course she has the luxury of picking the limes straight from her mom's tree in Key West! When I bit into her recipe for the first time, my mouth puckered so much it actually squirted! I know now that it's because she adds no sugar and adds one little bit extra juice at the end. Doing so makes a real difference in the tartness, if you don't want your mouth to pucker, leave out the extra teaspoon of limejuice!

3 egg yolks
1 can sweetened condensed milk
½ cup key lime juice, plus 1 tablespoon (fresh is much better than bottled)
1 Keebler brand graham cracker crust; or homemade

Preheat oven to 350°.

Combine the egg yolks with the condensed milk; beat until well blended. Add the juice and mix until thoroughly blended.

Bake the crust in the oven for 5 minutes and remove. Pour the pie filling into the crust, return to oven and bake 10 minutes. Cool on a wire rack and then refrigerate until cold.

Serve with fresh whipped cream if desired.

● ●

Sweet Potato Pie

I like sweet potato pie better than pumpkin; the topping gives it a crunchy sweetness that I adore!

Pie Crust:
10 large cinnamon graham crackers
1 cup pecan halves
¼ cup granulated sugar
1 Tbs. butter plus ½ stick butter; melted

Process the crackers, pecans, sugar and flour in your food processor until fine. Remove chopping blade and insert dough blade. Add butter and process on low until blended. Press mixture into a lightly greased 9" pie pan to form the crust.

Filling:
1 ¼ cups granulated sugar
½ Tbsp. ground cinnamon
½ tsp. ground nutmeg
2 eggs
1 12-ounce can evaporated milk
1 tsp. vanilla extract
1 ½ cups cooked and mashed sweet potatoes

In a mixing bowl, use your hand mixer to blend eggs, evaporated milk, vanilla and potatoes, until smooth. Add sugar and spices. Continue mixing until creamy. Pour into the prepared pie shell.

Topping:
1/3 cup butter or margarine
1/3 cup all-purpose flour
1/2 cup brown sugar, packed
1/2 cup shredded coconut
1/2 cup chopped pecans
Whipped topping or ice cream

Bake at 425° degrees for 15 minutes. Reduce heat to 350° degrees and bake for 30 minutes. Combine topping ingredients. Remove pie from the oven, sprinkle with topping. Continue baking 10-15 minutes or until topping is golden. Cool on rack. Refrigerate until cold and serve with whipped topping or ice cream.

• •

Peach Cobbler

To me, nothing is better than a good cobbler! I especially love peach cobbler, but I also like to mix fruits; like blackberry and peach or blueberry and apple! Make a cobbler using your favorite fruits, it easier than pie!

3 cups fresh or frozen cling peach sliced; thawed
1 cup sugar
1 cup flour
1 cup milk
1 teaspoon vanilla extract
¼ teaspoon salt
1 ½ tablespoon baking powder
1 cup sugar
1 stick butter

Mix fruit with 1 cup sugar; set aside. In mixing bowl, using your hand mixer, blend flour, milk, vanilla extract, salt, baking powder and remaining 1 cup sugar, on lowest speed, until thick; set aside.

Place the stick of butter into the bottom of a 9" x 9" x 4" pan and put into cool oven. Turn oven on and set to 350°. When butter has melted, remove pan from oven. Pour batter into pan with the butter; do not mix. Pour fruit and sugar mixture over all. Return to oven and bake for 1 hour.

This cobbler is delicious hot or cold, served alone or topped with cream, milk or ice cream.

Tropical 7-Up Cake

This cake is very good on a warm day when you want something sweet but a heavy frosted cake just seems too much!

1 18.25 ounce golden vanilla cake mix
¾ cup 7-Up
½ cup water
3 eggs
1/3 cup vegetable oil
1 8.25 ounce can pineapple chunks or tidbits; drained
1 11 ounce can mandarin orange segments; drained
½ cup shredded coconut; packed

Preheat oven to 350°. Lightly butter a 9x13-inch baking pan.

Blend together first 5 ingredients until smooth; pour into pan.

Mix the fruit and half of the coconut together and evenly distribute it over the batter. Bake for 20 minutes.

Remove from oven and sprinkle remaining coconut on top.

Return to oven and bake another 10 minutes or until cake is set, golden brown and the edges are just beginning to pull away from the sides of the pan.

Food Styling Tip

The cake will be prettier if you save about 1/3 of the pineapple and oranges to place atop the cake at the same time you add the extra coconut!

Big Mama's Boiled Custard

When I was very small, I remember my Grandmother, Big Mama (actually a very petite lady at 4' 11"!), making this in her outdoor kitchen, at her home by the lake in Georgia. She would serve it warm, in blue speckled ware mugs, and I thought it was the best thing in the whole world...I still do!

4 large eggs
1 cup sugar
1 quart milk
1/4 teaspoon salt
2 teaspoons vanilla

Warm milk, over low heat, in double boiler. Beat eggs in medium bowl; add sugar and beat thoroughly. Slowly add 2 cups of the warmed milk to egg mixture beating constantly.

Pour mixture into the double boiler with the remaining milk.

Gently cook over medium heat for 10-12 minutes; stirring constantly. DO NOT ALLOW MIXTURE TO BOIL. When the mixture thickly coats the spoon, remove from heat.

Stir in the vanilla. Strain the custard and pour into individual dessert dishes. Serve warm or refrigerate.

Food Styling Tip

After the custard has been poured into the dessert dishes, let it sit at room temperature until a skin barely begins to form on the top. Drop a slight pinch of nutmeg onto the top with your fingers. It should spread itself out across the surface. If you let it sit undisturbed for about 5 more minutes, the spice will form into the skin.

No-Bake Chocolate Oatmeal Cookies

I first made this recipe on HSN to demonstrate the power of my mixer, then I tasted it; it was love at first bite! I roll the cookies in shredded coconut for added color on camera, and because I like coconut, but you can omit this step if desired!

2 cups granulated sugar
3 tablespoons cocoa
1/4 cup butter
1/2 cup milk
3 cups oatmeal, quick cook style
1 teaspoon vanilla
1/2 cup peanut butter, homemade is best
1 cup shredded coconut

Place the sugar, cocoa, butter and milk into a medium saucepan and slowly bring to a gentle boil; stirring frequently. Remove from heat and allow to cool 5-10 minutes.

 In a large mixing bowl, use your hand mixer to combine the oatmeal, peanut butter and vanilla. Pour the warm chocolate mixture into the oatmeal mixture and continue to mix, on low, until everything is thoroughly combined.

While the mixture is still warm, form small balls and then roll them into the shredded coconut. Place on waxed paper and allow to cool completely.

Pecan Pralines

This is a great candy to make, put into small tins and pass out as gifts. Everyone loves it because it tastes great and it is a gift from the heart because you made it yourself!

1 cup sugar
1 cup brown sugar (½ light and ½ dark works best)
dash salt
½ cup milk
2 tablespoons white Karo syrup
2 tablespoons butter
1 teaspoon vanilla (real, not imitation)
1 ½ cups pecan halves

Mix the sugar, salt, milk and Karo syrup in a heavy 3-quart pan and cook until soft ball stage (the mixture will form a soft ball when you drop a little into cold water). Add butter and vanilla. Beat, using a hand mixer, until the mixture cools. Add pecans and drop by the tablespoon onto wax paper.

When firm, store in closed container. Makes about 2 dozen pralines.

Pecan Pie

So sweet and so rich, it is definitely one of my all-time favorites.

1 ¼ cups white Karo syrup
1 cup brown sugar
4 tablespoons butter
4 eggs
1 teaspoon vanilla
1 pound pecan halves
1 9-inch pie shell; unbaked

Preheat oven to 350º.

Bring Karo syrup and brown sugar to a boil in a medium saucepan. Add butter. Remove from heat and beat in eggs. Add vanilla and stir well.

Pour mixture into pie shell. Place the pecan halves on top of the filling, forming decorative circles from the outer edge inward.

Bake for 45 minutes.

Remove from oven and cool on a wire rack. Serve at room temperature or cold. Top with whipped cream if desired.

Old-Fashioned Strawberry Shortcake

My Father's side of the family is from Plant City, Fl; strawberry capital of the world! I once ate so much strawberry shortcake at the Strawberry Festival; I was expecting my daughter at the time, that I didn't eat strawberries for 5 years! However, you can't give up something so good forever!

When you want to impress your guests, serve this! Not those store-bought sponge cakes, but the real thing!

1/3 cup shortening
¾ cup whole milk
1 egg
2 ½ cups flour
1 teaspoon salt
4 teaspoons baking powder
1 tablespoon sugar
1 quart ripe strawberries; sliced and sweetened with 1 cup sugar
1 pint whipping cream; whipped with 1 tablespoon sugar

Preheat oven to 325°.

Put all the dry ingredients together and soft into a large mixing bowl. Mix the shortening into the flour, blend the egg into milk and then mix together with the flour mixture to form a dough. Put onto a lightly floured surface and knead until smooth.

Divide the dough into two parts. Pat or roll out half the dough to fit a 9" cake pan. Place into the pan and sprinkle generously with flour. Pat or roll out the other half of the dough and place on top of the other dough. Bake until done; about 30 minutes.

When cool enough to handle, separate the layers. Place the bottom layer on a cake plate. Spread with half of the sweetened berries and cover with half of the whipped cream. Put on the top layer and spread with the remaining berries (except one or two to use as garnish) and then the remaining whipped cream. Add the saved garnish berries to the top!

Chocolate Cherry Chip Cookies

These cookies are festive to look at and wonderful to eat. That is why I make them on HSN during the holiday season! Just be careful to add the cocoa a little at a time so it doesn't dust your counters and your clothes!

1 cup light brown sugar (firmly packed)
1 ½ cups granulated sugar
4 sticks of margarine
4 large eggs
½ cup Cocoa
1 ½ tsp. vanilla
4 ½ cups all-purpose flour
1 tablespoon baking soda
1 tablespoon baking powder
1 ½ cups white chocolate chips
1 cup (8 oz.) candied cherries; coarsely chopped
1 cup coarsely chopped walnuts

In a large bowl, beat the sugars, margarine, eggs and vanilla until creamy using your hand mixer. Switch mixer to low speed and slowly add in the Cocoa until well blended. Add the flour, baking soda and baking powder and mix until cookie dough is smooth. Remove beaters and insert dough hooks. Add the cherries, chips and nuts; blend just until mixed.

Drop rounded teaspoons of dough onto an un-greased cookie sheet. Bake at 350° for 8-10 minutes or until light golden brown.

Let cool on cookie sheet for 5 minutes and then transfer to a cooling rack. Store cookies in an airtight container.

See **Food Styling Tip** under the Everything Cookie recipe on page 211.

Index

224

A Quick Lesson on Food Styling

There are too many tricks of the trade, if you are Food Styling for photographs or other professional publications, to go into in just a page or two; in fact whole books are dedicated to the subject. For the purpose of this book, I will give tips to you, the home cook, which you may use to make the appearance of you food more beautiful to look at without hurting the flavor of the dish!

- Always choose the freshest, firmest produce with vibrant color and free of blemishes. Smaller is often better!

- When buying poultry, insist that the butcher open any visually impairing packaging and personally inspect the skin. Do not accept poultry that has tears or rips in the skin if the breast, or splits in the skin by the cavity opening!

- Red meats should be lean and well trimmed.

- Seafood should be firm and of good color. Refuse any seafood that has a sheen or opaque color.

- While preparing the ingredients, use a very sharp knife and a clean work-surface.

- Make cuts and slices uniformly and as large as you can without hurting the integrity of the dish. For example, when cutting peppers you would, ideally, cut them in like-sized length-wise strips. If they must be diced, try to leave them as large as you can. You want to be able to see them!

- When cooking the foods, stir, flip and mix them gently and infrequently; do not mash and tear the foods.

- Cook foods only until just done to the taste; do not cook them until they are mushy and colorless!

- When making pasta salads or other dishes that call for "raw" vegetables like broccoli, green beans, cauliflower and zucchini, blanch them in boiling water for 1 minute and them plunge them into ice water and refrigerate until you are ready to add them to your dish. The blanching will give the veggies a much more vibrant color!

- Pastas should be cooked Al Dente and then rinsed with water to wash away the sticky starch. Then toss with a little oil!

- When cooking meats for stews, pot roasts or in a slow cooker, the dish will look much better if the meat is browned first! Rub the meat with oil and sear quickly in a very hot pan, making sure to get all sides equally browned. Then place the meat into the cooking vessel and go from there. Any thing sweet like brown sugar, honey, syrup and even Coca Cola, will aid in the browning, so if you are preparing a food that you do not want to overcook by browning, like chicken or fish, rub with a mixture of oil and a browning agent. This will also work on the grill to make grill marks!

- Sauté foods in a combination of equal parts butter to oil (use good, light colored oil) will produce a better appearance than butter alone as butter will burn and darken the food.

- When serving your meals, color is key! Enhance your dishes by adding garnishes or seasonings of a contrasting color. A little parsley does wonders! Or, choose a fresh flower or a slice of fruit! Garnish does not have to make sense from a culinary stand point as no one should eat it, so even pretty leaves, nuts and berries from your trees outside will bring a nice touch to the table.

- Be mindful of the dish you choose to serve the food in; for example, don't put chicken on a yellow plate unless you are placing a bed of lettuce, sliced oranges or cherry tomatoes under or around it! Blue or green plates work well with most foods, as does white; the choice of many restaurants!

- Height adds great visual interest to foods. Try to mound foods high in a small area rather than to spread food out; for example, use an ice-cream scoop to serve mashed potatoes, and lean the steak on it's side against it! Think of a plate as the base to build a pyramid!

- Don't forget the edge of the plate! Sprinkle herbs or drizzle sauce on it to add a gourmet touch.

I hope some of these tips will help you prepare and serve dishes you are proud to present to the eyes as well as to the palettes!

Personal Notes & Recipes

When you want to make changes to my recipes, add new recipes from HSN.com or if you see products or demonstrations on-air that you would like more information on, jot them down here! That way, you'll always have them handy!

Personal Notes & Recipes

Personal Notes & Recipes

Be sure to logon to HSN.com for the latest Bravetti products and current recipe offerings!

To comment about this cookbook or to make suggestions regarding up-coming books, please write to me at adscutte@tampabay.rr.com.